# This Robot Brain Gets Life (Making AI Pseudo-Conscious)

*Design Alignment In, Design Hallucination Out*

*(Book II in the Sentience series)*

# This Robot Brain Gets Life (Making AI Pseudo-Conscious)

*Design Alignment In, Design Hallucination Out*

*(Book II in the Sentience series)*

## Carter Blakelaw

## The Logic of Dreams

This Robot Brain Gets Life (Making AI Pseudo-Conscious): *Design Alignment In, Design Hallucination Out*

Book II in the Sentience series

First print edition. April 2023.

ISBN paperback: 979-8-3921426-1-3

ISBN hardback (dust cover): 978-1-7396887-9-0

Published by The Logic of Dreams

Requests to publish work from this book should be sent to:

toolbox@carterblakelaw.com

While every precaution has been taken in the preparation of this book, the publisher assumes no responsibility for errors or omissions, or for damages resulting from the use of the information contained herein.

Cover art, book design and illustrations by Jack Calverley.

Photography by Mick Haupt and Bruno Figueiredo from www.unsplash.com.

10 9 8 7 6 5 4 3 2 1

**www.TheLogicOfDreams.com**

t-37-pb

### *There Is Only One Sun*

There is only one Sun;
You can't copy the blazing
Light in the sky
And make another one.
There is only one Sun;
You cannot tear a piece off,
Return to Earth,
And have a second one spun.
There is only one Sun;
You cannot paint its like,
Cannot start a fire even half as bright
For even at night you depend on its light.
There is only one Sun.

C.B. 2023

Dedicated to the memory of Tommy Slack, Jim and Cecilia's eldest

# Contents

# Introduction

I will keep this short.
- To align an AI's goals with our own, we must build-in alignment from the start,
- To keep an AI honest, we must build-in honesty from the start,
- To get an AI to understand anything, we must invest it with something of what it's like to be conscious but, as you will see, it does not have to go the whole hog.

In this book, a theory of consciousness is cast into an AI architecture that allows interventions in the device's thought processes—*by design*.

As in the first book in this series (The Man in My Head Has Lost His Mind, Logic of Dreams, 2023) there are two principles that frame our approach:
- Occam's Razor (in short: go for the simplest solution),
- The need to expunge the homunculus from all activity.

And just what is this *homunculus*?

Traditionally, this homunculus is a small man who is concealed inside an otherwise inert machine and controls the machine to give the impression that the machine is alive or intelligent[1].

In science, when we fail to explain properly how something works and instead explain a thing in terms of

---

1     E.g. The Mechanical Turk a chess machine hoax constructed by Wolfgang von Kempelen dating from 1770.

a magical process X that does all the difficult stuff, we can be said to be relying on a homunculus (i.e. process X).

Suppose you were to ask me: "How do you add numbers in your head, like for instance 5 plus 7?"

And I were to answer: "I rely on a natural brain process called *Perplexia* which simply brings the answer to my lips."

Then I would be appealing to a mysterious, magical homunculus, the process *Perplexia*, and I would be explaining nothing.

The risk in attempting to explain anything related to the brain or the mind[2] is that a homunculus can all too easily creep into what seems like a perfectly reasonable explanation.

If you were to ask me: "How do we perceive the color red?"

I might answer: "Light of a certain frequency stimulates cells at the back of the eye and ultimately leads to the activation of neurons that give rise to the color red."

The problem with my explanation is that I have not explained how we arrive at our *perception* of the color red. I have merely confined the difficulty of generating perceptions to the activities of 'activated neurons' ('activated neurons' being the homunculi here).

Put another way, I have *begged the question* originally asked. How do we perceive the color red? By perceiving the color red.

Well, that question-begging homunculus is the devil which, in this book, I will studiously expunge.


So much for the *methodology* that I will use in the pages that follow. But what of the task itself?

At least part of the point of this book is that you cannot

---

2       Like meaning and understanding, both of which we need to explore if we want to construct a thinking machine.

retrofit honesty and morality to an artificial intelligence because honesty and morality[3] require homunculi[4] to deliver them.

Must human beings police every possible output from every one of these wayward AIs[5] or are we going to build homunculi to do the job for us?

If the former, there will always be human error and imperfect human-designed systems letting bad stuff escape (aside from the size of the workforce involved).

If the latter: what would be the point when any artificial homunculus capable of delivering honesty and morality should easily out-perform its deceitful, amoral AI cousins?

The answer must be to build a better AI to begin with. To understand enough to build the homunculus we want and need, and forget about retrofitting anything.

Let us treat the first incursion into the realm of Big AI as the cul-de-sac it is, and travel a different path.

In this book I develop the architecture and principles that will deliver the thinking machine we need.

Is this a technical book?

Well now *that* is a difficult question!

This book is about ideas, and about one idea in particular: how a machine can think. This involves smidgens of philosophy and psychology and some ideas from computer engineering. But for those that might worry about the book's being too technical, I offer Figure 0, The One Idea.

---

3    Being complex and nuanced things and the bane of philosophers.
4    With regard to honesty and morality, we humans are those full-bodied homunculi.
5    Or invent and forever be fiddling with and bringing up to date preemptive bad behaviour prevention mechanisms. We all know what software updates are like.

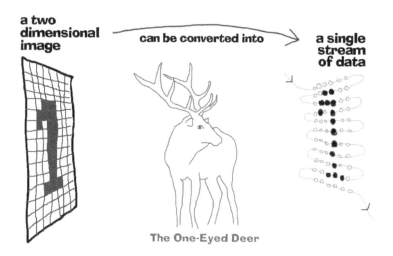

**a two dimensional image** — can be converted into → **a single stream of data**

The One-Eyed Deer

Figure 0. The One Idea.

So long as you see that we can take the image held in a two-dimensional grid and convert it to a one-dimensional data stream, you should be able to follow all the reasoned arguments and ideas and examples in this text (bad puns notwithstanding).

If you understand the principle illustrated in Figure 0, that a two dimensional image can be translated into a single stream of data, then I think you should be able to grasp anything I present between the covers of this book.

My claim is to have an answer to the question: "Does a machine need to be conscious to think about the world?" And, given the insights gained from developing the architecture of one such machine, I go on to explain how we can design-in honesty and morality from the get-go.

So, *is this a technical book?*

If your curiosity drives you, then nothing in what follows will stop you following.

How's that for an answer?

*CB April 2023*

# 1. The Woods and the Tree

Friday afternoons at school were spent on a special activity.

For me, on this particular Friday, that meant coppicing a small overgrown thicket that lay between the school playing fields and the grazing land of a neighbouring farm.

You may know that coppicing involves cropping the narrow trunks of young trees close to the ground in the expectation that the stump will sprout new shoots while at the same time letting the sun penetrate the tree canopy all the way down to the light-deprived earth, to encourage biodiversity at ground level. Meaning: today we were set to cut down a bunch of small trees.

Our little team involved a teacher (he too had been 'assigned' a special Friday afternoon activity), myself (carrying a bow saw), and another boy (carrying a bill-hook).

It was an all-boys school, if you're wondering, and this isn't a crime story so although I mention the bill-hook to help sketch the scene, the bill-hook won't be heard of again.

I should mention that I had been assigned to a similar special activity in a similarly neglected patch of school land the previous year. The teacher had not.

As every school-age pupil must surely know (having learnt such things from animated cartoon films) to cut down a tree you first cut a horizontal V in the trunk on the side you want the tree to fall, then make a simple horizontal cut on the other side, most of the way through,

1

and then gently, standing well back, encourage the tree to move in the direction you want it to fall, hoping that the canopy of branches of neighbouring trees is not so dense as to trap and hold the newly liberated trunk more or less vertically.

(This is not an instruction manual, mind you. So please don't try this at home. Always employ a professional, take precautions, get life insurance, etc. etc.—you know what I'm saying.)

So far, so good. I set to with the bow saw about a palm's width above ground level, and cut the horizontal V. The teacher and other student stood safely away from where the tree was expected to fall.

I set about making the single horizontal cut on the far side from the V and, with the tree creaking and swaying a little, I withdrew the saw and looked expectantly at the teacher.

"Cut it all the way through," he said.

I explained that if I did so, the tree would slip back and trap the blade of the saw.

"Cut it!"

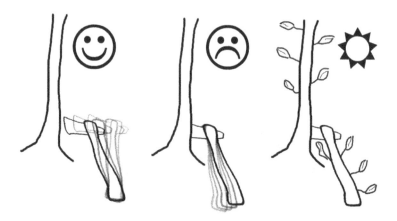

**Forestry fumbled and foiled**

Figure 1. Managing the environment.

I cut all the way through. The liberated trunk slid back, trapped the blade of the saw, and hung in the air, held upright by the canopy.

"I suppose you're going to say 'I told you so,'" the teacher said.

"No." In all honesty that was not the thought that crossed my mind. My thoughts were more observational than judgemental, more curious than unkind (although obviously since I so clearly remember the incident, it must have had some impact on me).

*And so what?* Say you.

*So this...* Say I.

In my mind I had formed an impression of the task at hand. I had short-term goals: to cut the V, cut the horizontal, and to push. I had an expectation that the trunk would readily break at a certain uncut thickness and fall in a certain direction. These impressions occupied my mind before and during the attempt to cut down the tree.

The teacher had a different set of impressions and expectations, which were not borne out by reality.

Some might say that I had more *learnt experience* to draw upon; the teacher, being new to the task, had none.

What my anecdote does though, is draw attention to three missing elements in the Lock Step model of consciousness developed in *The Man In My Head Has Lost His Mind* [Logic of Dreams 2023, hereinafter referred to as MIMH].

In that book, the Lock Step model Mark I presents consciousness as seated at the junction where the brain's best guess at what the external world is like meets whatever evidence the brain has gleaned from the senses (Figure 2).

This is an abstract model, bearing no direct resemblance to the way the brain works. It gives an account of what we are conscious of, but it offers little by way of explanation as to how we might anticipate events

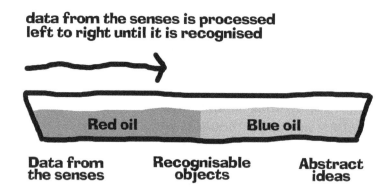

Figure 2. The Lock Step model Mark I [from MIMH]. The two oils represent (i) red—the passage of data from the senses as it is processed and (ii) blue—the speculative construction of a best-guess model of the world.

in the physical world, like the falling of the tree, or how we initiate actions, like cutting a 'V', and the model is entirely silent on how we might imagine impossible things, or have new ideas.

On the left hand side of the Lock Step model (the red oil in the tray) we have sensory data transiting a substrate as it travels towards the right, being processed to ever greater abstraction. On the right hand side (the blue oil in the tray) we have vague and abstract representations transiting the substrate towards the left, becoming ever more specific. Where the two oils meet, and settle in an uneasy equilibrium, we find the best fit between expectation and available evidence, and there we say consciousness resides.

But in this model there is no leeway to invent new thoughts, thoughts about things that don't exist. All you can do is travel the substrate[1]. You envisage the falling of a tree: how does the model cope with that? You impel the saw to cut a slot in the tree trunk: how does the model cope with that?

---

1          Albeit modifying it a little as you go to capture frequently experienced patterns.

Not only must a successful model cope with these scenarios, but it must also comply with Occam's Razor (applied here to mean: keep it simple).

In particular, we have manifested numerous variations of our personal concept of 'a tree'—standing up, falling down, resting on a saw blade. How many concepts of tree do I need to store in my head? Regardless of how I store the concept of 'a tree', I should not be storing any single piece of brain-data more than once in my physical brain[2]. That means that if the brain serves up the memory of a tree, I must use that same brain-based memory when I anticipate the tree's coming down. Otherwise, if the same memory were to exist in two locations, how would they be kept in synchronisation[3]?

Does this mean that the same area of brain substrate is somehow involved in all the remembering, the anticipating, and the taking of action?

This we will have to think about.

In a way one might say that the Lock Step model is OK as far as it goes, but it is so remote from the real brain that it tells us nothing of deeper interest: there is no mathematical or conceptual mapping, or translation, from the Lock Step model to a real physical brain.

How might one develop the model to bring it closer to

---

2    The concept of a tree is most likely structured, of course, and will be hierarchical and many-branched. A tree is not one concept, but many connected concepts i.e. to cater for species, variety, age, seasonal variation, and composition, including bark, seed and leaves. But to whatever extent we end up breaking down our concept of 'a tree', the individual elements we are ultimately left with should not be duplicated in brain storage.

3    The two memories of the same thing would have to be kept in synchronization with one another because, while memories may change, may become more or less elaborate, or vague, we do not experience memories as flip-flop alternatives: On Mondays, Wednesdays, and Fridays I believe I grew up in a family of four in a high rise; On Tuesdays, Thursdays, and Saturdays I believe I grew up in a family of seven on a farm. Sometimes we forget, true, but a memory's sometimes being inaccessible (aided by wine or whatever) is different from having two memories of the 'same' thing. We simply don't. Somehow the mechanism of memory allocation and memory recall (if and when it works at all) achieves uniqueness. Any syncing could fail.

reality, to make it useful and applicable, to make such a mapping, as it were, transparent, and possible?

Well that is part of the mission of this book: I invite you to consider, if you will, the proposition that we build a general purpose thinking machine (an AI), leaning heavily on the Lock Step model, which behaves much like a brain, except that it lacks consciousness (because it has no *gleeon* capture mechanism as per the theory proposed in MIMH). By working through the necessary features of such a machine we might hope to find our mapping and benefit from the insights that the machine and the process of designing it reveal.

A part also of the mission of this book is to think about how such a machine might work, and how we might operate it so that it does not make the mistake the teacher made.

Armed with these ideas, one might hope to implement such a machine in any material: whether steam-powered and driving gears, or springs and clockwork, or racks and rows of electronic valves, or as one might expect these days, microscopically, as transistors on silicon chips—or one might merely simulate it in software...

Ultimately, we are after a physical mechanism that entertains ideas but is not conscious.

What kind of architecture could our machine possibly have?

Indeed, are we to imagine a brain-machine (just like the tray in the Lock Step model) consisting of a massive number of uniformly distributed calculating units that carpet the bottom of the tray?

Each unit would need to be able to perform one of several operations depending on whether it was being required to process incoming data from the senses (covered by red oil), or to generate the anticipated data from the deep unconscious (covered by blue oil) or even, where the two notional oils meet and the two streams

a) **Many Processes run across some shared region of substrate in many directions**

b) **Separate input output, memory and sandbox blocks**

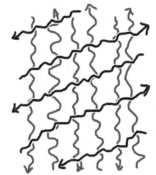

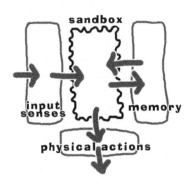

Figure 3. (a) Uniform, generic processing substrate versus (b) specialized regions.

of data are matched, to generate consciousness (or its equivalent)? Figure 3a.

Or are we to think of different regions of the brain-machine as serving separate purposes? One region exclusively processes incoming data from the senses; another region exclusively stores memories; and we introduce a 'sandbox' region for general purpose processing which is able to copy the contents from the perception region, or from memory, and make what sense it can of them? Figure 3b.

In this text I will briefly explore both approaches to implementing the Lock Step model before deciding on the most promising and pursuing that to its logical terminus. But it is my intention, in building the model, to leave out the final stage in which consciousness is generated[4]. If successful, I will refer to the machine as *pseudo-conscious*. That is to say: a machine which could be

---

4        As per MIMH, consciousness would have to be designed-in as a *gleeon* capture mechanism.

expected to behave much as a human being might behave *sans* consciousness, but with a few specific motivations.

Such a machine (as per MIMH Chapter 7) would not be attuned to pain, or joy, or fear, or the rest. A machine which, I posit, could not be a victim of ethical or unethical treatment because it is not conscious. By the same token such a machine could not be blamed for ethical or unethical behaviour. Blame (or praise) for any ethical or unethical acts performed by the machine should reside with the creator of the machine, the builder, and also with the trainers, instructors and operators. It would be as if we were dealing with the designer, manufacturer, owner and operator of a car, each of whom should be fully accountable for the consequences of what they do, for the part they play, for the contribution they make...

As to my role, and motivation, and culpability[5] in presenting the ideas that I do in pages such as these: I am driven by a desire to know—by curiosity[6]. I hope to use reason to tease out some truths about the world, about us, and about the machines we choose to make. How can something that is essentially mechanical grasp something that is essentially conceptual? Must we not inform ourselves better for the choices that we all face? In doing so we might hope to identify pinch-points in the design of machines such as those suggested in these pages, in order that we might incorporate effective and timely safety measures.

So, let us develop the Lock Step model, turn it into something real and (if you will forgive a little grotesque *Hollywoodesque* hyperbole): explore the edge of consciousness.

---

5        Having introduced a moral element, it would be wrong for me to duck the question myself.

6        The Deckard character (Harrison Ford) in the movie Blade Runner (1982, dir. Ridley Scott) asks the Tyrell character (Joe Turkel) in reference to Racheal, an android (Sean Young): 'How can it not know what it is?'

Can we, as humans, answer that same question about ourselves? If not, why not? What is stopping us?

As for that Friday all those years ago and the coppice in the making, I have not been back to check whether the work was repeated as it should have been, every so many years. Quite possibly, of course, any such patch of empty land has been gobbled up for some other purpose, being as it is, or was, so close to space-starved London.

And as for the teacher, I think, as I write this, he must be long-retired.

Nonetheless, the tree-felling decision will serve as a litmus test for the effectiveness of the computing device that I present over the course of the pages that follow.

## 2. An All-in-One Supercell

The dancing cats at The Jellicle Ball in *Cats*™ the musical[1] start to dance:

In gentle synchronisation they sway, paw the ground, and stretch. A whispering chorus announces The Ball; the cats flex and pirouette. They bow to the ground and reach up to a dark, glittering sky, then settle back and close in upon themselves into nervous bundles of taut flesh to stalk an invisible prey. A sudden shatter-glass noise and, shocked, they break formation and scatter. Now each cat prowls in its own complex, gyrating way, fearfully eyeing a stage that is set for a night of nerve-jangling drama...

The dancers' moves are complex and memorised. These are moves for which, much of the time, the only prompt is the music. And yet each dancer must be aware of what the next dancer in line is doing; each must know, and sense, how their timing and their posture compares; aware of the space they are able to occupy without collision.

As they go through their moves, each dancer is essentially independent, performing a complex memorised routine but fitting it to a synchronised pattern when required.

Let us switch our attention to the sky in daylight and a flock of geese flying in V-formation.

Each goose in the flock is far more dependent on what its near neighbour is doing. A goose will position itself

---

1    Cats is a trademark of The Really Useful Group Ltd.

to get extra lift from the airflow around the wing of the bird ahead of it. This aid to lift is optimal just behind and to one side of the bird in front. Thus, naturally, each bird will find the place of minimum effort and the flock will automatically organise itself into V formation[2]. To arrive at the formation each bird has only to notice the position in the air where they need to exert themselves the least.

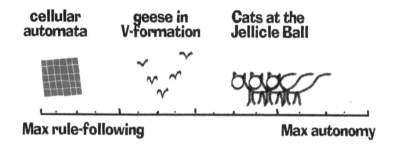

## Along the scale of co-operating processors showing more or less co-operation

Figure 4. Along the scale of co-operating processors.

The birds appear to follow a rule which they have copied or discovered (and which is reinforced by experience. So it is reasonable to think that these birds, having brains, after a short time will naturally choose to adopt such a flight arrangement; meaning they are following a rule).

While the dancers in *Cats* have autonomy and choose sometimes to dance independently and sometimes in synchronisation, the geese have autonomy but are motivated to keep to a rule and always fly in formation.

If we think of these greater or lesser rule-based behaviours as occupying two positions on a scale which

---

2        The V shape is developed rather than a diamond shape because there is turbulence from any bird already flying directly ahead.

itself ranges from pure rule-based conformity at one end, to pure autonomy at the other, then at the furthest rule-following end of the scale we have what are called *cellular automata*. These are (essentially) mathematical entities. Typically they might be represented as pixels on a screen and might be programmed (say) to react exclusively to the state of their closest neighbours.

Let us suppose that the automata sit on a rectangular grid (as per a computer or smart-phone screen). Each pixel-automaton has four directly adjacent neighbours and four obliquely adjacent neighbours. Suppose these automata can exist in one of two states. Let's label the states 1 and 0. A rule might be (say) to add together the state values of direct neighbours and subtract the state values of oblique neighbours. If the total is greater than 0 an automaton enters the '1' state, otherwise it enters the '0' state. Some initial pattern of 1s and 0s is imposed upon the array of automata, and the array is clocked, which is to say, every cell computes its next state and then changes to that next state. Once one clock action is complete, the

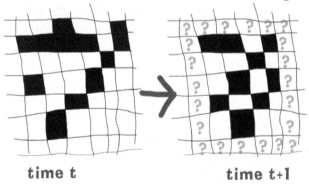

time t                                        time t+1

rule: add adjacent, subtract oblique
     if result is greater than 0,
     then assign 1, otherwise assign 0
     (black is 1, white is 0)

Figure 5. Cellular automata obey a simple rule to arrive at their next clocked state. At the edge of the grid we might decide that missing cells all contribute (say) 0, but that decision will depend on how we want our automata to end up behaving.

array is clocked again.

If an observer sees 1s as dark pixels and 0s as light pixels then, as the array is clocked, the initial pattern will be seen to morph into something new (Figure 5), or possibly will go all dark, or all light.

In *Cats*, with geese, and with cellular automata we have examples of how a region (a stage, an airspace, or a computer screen) might be uniformly populated by a single species of processor which, when replicated across the region, with more or less rule-keeping, may produce widely different, non-uniform results.

This is the idea behind the introduction of a generic processor, uniformly distributed, and uniformly connected, across a notional brain-like substrate, as per Figure 3a. After all, when we think of the brain—when we look at a physical brain—it appears to be formed from a single kind of stuff, greyish-white and crinkly. Even under the lens over relatively large areas it seems fairly consistently composed of the things it's composed of. It is not unreasonable to wonder whether it all—like an ant in an anthill or bee in a beehive—works in the same way; a repeated pattern of cells or cell structures which, after all, was the original motivation behind the perceptron[3] and the original artificial neural networks.


Let us delve into the Lock Step model in a little more depth with a view to finding a generic processor with which to populate the whole substrate.

In the Lock Step model we have a tray that contains two adjacent pools of oil, one red and one blue (Figure 2).

---

3        The perceptron was invented in 1943 by McCulloch and Pitts. It is a calculating unit (or cell) with several inputs and a single output and was intended to mimic the action of a neuron to the extent that neurons were understood at the time. The output is calculated from the inputs and an artificial neural network of perceptrons can be constructed and tuned so that the network as a whole can recognize patterns in the inputs, and thereby serve to recognize images or other patterns in pattern-bearing data.

The oils meet to form a line roughly midway along the tray. The junction where the two meet forms a thin ribbon that we can visualise as lying on its edge across the width of the tray. We can think of the two oils ebbing and flowing along the length of the tray, moved by the micro-hairs that line the bottom[4]. And since we think of the ribbon junction as the seat of consciousness, we can think of attention and mental focus shifting to and fro, settling now on this, now on that interpreted feature of the sensory world, guided by the micro-hairs, which in turn we think of as standing for the substrate of the brain[5] as it seeks to maximise meaning [MIMH Chapter 5].

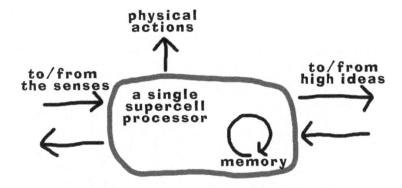

Figure 6. The Supercell. An attempt to implement a substrate that mimics the uniformity of the Lock Step tray model. The substrate would be populated with thousands of these supercells, each connected to at least two neighbours.

Into this model let us introduce the supercell (Figure 6), which is our own version of a cellular automaton. Let us introduce a large number of them, distributed evenly and interconnected across the entire substrate.

---

4        ...and the two oils are magically kept level, for the sake of the thought experiment, by pumping oil in at one end, and out from the other, as needed to make the thought experiment work.

5        Being non-specific here and using substrate to mean all the neurons, glial etc. cells, i.e. not committing to any particular basis as to what supports consciousness.

Reminding ourselves: on the far left hand side of the tray (red) we have direct data input from the senses. On the far right hand side of the tray (blue) the data represents very general, abstract ideas. These data signals are passed from supercell to supercell, in both directions at once, across the entire substrate, and acted on by each supercell in passing.

Now, if these supercells are to implement the Lock Step oil tray model, we need each supercell to compare the two data streams, and for the data to be transformed in a useful way as it passes through.

While the Lock Step model envisages data being transformed as it propagates in both directions, looking at the detail we may only need data to be transformed in one direction of travel. For instance, the data coming from the right.

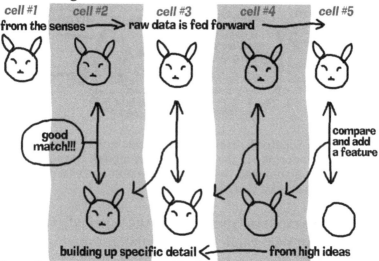

Figure 7. An image is processed by five supercells, in both directions.

The most abstract form of the animal face is a circle (in cell #5). As the circle is processed right to left, detail is added to it, making it more specific, until the best match is found in cell #2.

Each of the features which is added must either be a generic shape (like a line or curve, specified inside the supercell) or a learnt shape, taken from memory.

So, in this instance, when each cell compares the two data streams and finds no match[6], the data in the high level/abstract stream is made more specific by recognising some feature in the sensory data stream from the left and adding the recognised feature to the stream coming from the right, before sending the modified data leftwards (Figure 7)[7].

We do however rely on memory for feature recognition because any feature could occur at any position across the substrate (the cat's head might move). Every supercell must have access to every memory.

So while this picture captures the spirit of the Lock Step oil tray model, it becomes difficult to see how the memory of features and of fully-formed objects can be incorporated unless memory is treated as a separate functional block, external to the supercell substrate.

If we are forced to have a separate memory block, and still lack any explanation of imagination, prediction, or deliberate action, let us see if we can fare better in the next chapter with the block architecture of Figure 3b.

---

6        If the data streams match, we can temporarily pause our search along this stream of data and claim we have our best guess at what the external world is really like, and switch on consciousness (or pseudo-consciousness) for the current data representation at the current location.

7        In this illustration we ignore data bandwidth and dimensionality. We are looking for a mechanism that, in the general principle of its operation, might work.

## 3. There Is Only One Sun

*There is only one Sun;*
*You can't copy the blazing*
*Light in the sky*
*And make another one.*
*There is only one Sun;*
*You cannot tear a piece off,*
*Return to Earth,*
*And have a second one spun.*
*There is only one Sun;*
*You cannot paint its like,*
*Cannot start a fire even half as bright*
*For even at night you depend on its light.*
*There is only one Sun.*

In my youth, I spent two weeks of the long vacation with cousins on the small-holding that was their home.

And I have a clear memory of their goat, standing on its hind legs with its front feet planted on some vehicle or other as it tore leaves from the lower branches of a small tree. I watched, amused, with one of the cousins—though whether this was Tommy or Matthew or James, I don't recall.

Shortly, one of the adults emerged from the house and shooed the goat from the vehicle and rebuked us for allowing the goat to misbehave.

But the clear image that remains is of the goat on its hind legs, tucking into the tree. I cannot tell you what the vehicle was, nor whether the goat risked denting bonnet (hood) or boot (trunk). Maybe after a session of reminiscences I would be able to correctly elaborate

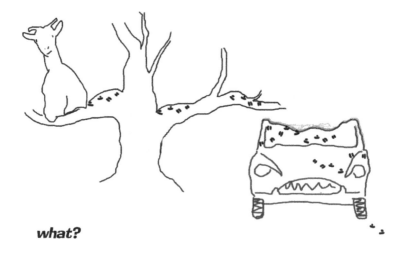

**what?**

Figure 8. The innocence of the goat.

my memory, and no doubt my memory would change to incorporate the new information. Memories are not immutable things, that much I know. Except that it would still be *that* memory. The memory of *that* goat using some vehicle or other to reach the leaves.

Even were the details of the recollection to be changed by subsequent discussion with those who were there at the time, the amended memory would still be the memory of the goat. I would not create a second memory: in the first, the car is a DAF; in the second, the car is a Mini—or whatever. I am simply vague about the make of vehicle. In my mind, as I think back now, it was merely a vehicle the goat could get purchase on in order to reach higher than it might unaided. The family had a DAF (I recall it being automatic and belt-driven) and they had a Mini (I recall that as having front wheel drive). It was probably one of those, I think, when I think about it, but maybe not[1]. Regardless, every time I reference it, it is that one

1      Further rummaging through my memories makes me think it might in fact have been the family's VW Campervan, making the goat something of a mountain goat, but also better explaining the ire of the adult.

single memory that I fetch from the invisible store in my brain, to reveal to my mind—the goat on its hind legs.

There is only one Sun.

Even if the Sun were blue, even if its light were half as bright; even if its pull on us were twice as strong; there is only one Sun. And, somehow, the rememberings that make up my memory are like that.

So when we put to one side the idea from the previous chapter of a substrate uniformly populated by supercells, and add memory to our model as a separate functional block (alongside  sandbox, sensory input, and physical actions, Figure 3b), we will need to treat memory as a pool of unique recollections that can be individually inserted, extracted, and changed[2].

Let's not forget that we are trying to map the very general, illustrative model of the Lock Step oil tray to a logically similar, functional architecture that plausibly might entertain ideas and would not make the tree-felling error made by the teacher mentioned in Chapter 1. Most likely, the physical organisation of real biological brains will turn out to be very different from our functional overview. In real brains Nature (via evolution) will likely have packed cells as tightly as possible for the sake of minimising both the energy required to operate them and the nutrients required to grow and sustain them and their connections.

Caveats notwithstanding, here are some functionalities in our brain-ish Lock Step tray for which we might usefully seek analogues:

**Feature #1**: Electrochemical signals from the senses are continually sieved for patterns and shapes, and these signals, patterns and shapes are processed to the highest

---

2      And while memories may be false, or adjusted, or warped, in a healthy brain we must assume that the mechanism does not fail; it works as it needs to in an ever-changing world, and it works by not duplicating memories. This is an experiment you can perform for yourself. I ask, is there any single event in your life that you remember as two distinct occurrences?

order general representations that can be extracted from them,

**Feature #2**: Electrochemical signals from a concept-forming region are continually generated and adjusted, and represent speculations about what the world is like, and what it contains (the wider context, as we conceive of it, and the objects in that context),

**Feature #3**: Where the two streams of signals meet, and match, we have consciousness[3]. In a minimum configuration, it is from the region of consciousness that new memories are laid down (or old ones adjusted) because, in the Lock Step model, for consciousness to make an evolutionary difference, it must be able to lay down and alter memories[4] [MIMH Chapter 7].

There are three factors that we ought also to contemplate at some point, though perhaps not immediately.

**Factor #1**: Neurons are uni-directional (dendrite to axon),

**Factor #2**: Memory formation is generally considered to involve arrangements (topologies) of dendrite connections,

**Factor #3**: We have yet to give any account of intentional (muscular or otherwise) actions.

Let us start again, from scratch, with our transformation from the Lock Step model to a workable brain-ish architecture.

In Figure 9 we have expanded awareness from the ribbon junction of the Lock Step tray to a processing block in its own right. This is based on the intuition that if we have two broad neural paths accepting traffic in opposite

---

3       We would also add, since in the Lock Step model the ribbon of consciousness follows attention, and attention follows maximum meaning from one instant to the next, some measure of maximum mental activity is also involved, and correlates to focus of attention.
4       Besides, do you have any memories which you acquired without ever being aware of the events that gave rise to them?

directions, and if these two paths are unidirectional, fixed and static, then a separate block must be introduced to provide an adjustable mechanism for attention, which can shift its focus to and fro along either path, and compare the contents of the two.

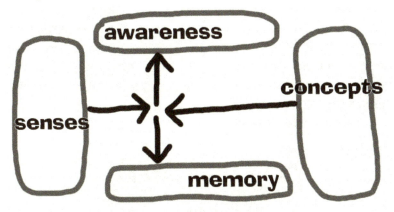

Figure 9. First broad blocky generalisation derived from the Lock Step model.

However this model is obviously lacking because we have no means to read from memory, so we tweak the model to become Figure 10, in which memories are made available on the concept side to assist with concept formation.

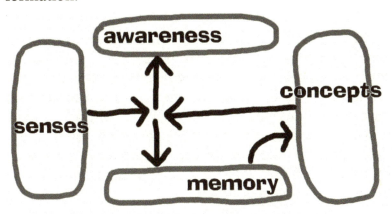

Figure 10. Allow memory to help with concept formation.

In Figure 10 we present awareness as acting like a puppet-master; we might envisage strings attached from the awareness block to every step along both of the two arrows between the sense-side and concept-side blocks. However, use of a separate block of such puppet-master awareness is unnecessary[5]. We could make the concept block dynamic, no longer thinking of it as an extension of the senses block where the direction of data flow has been reversed. Instead we could envisage the concept block as working in an entirely different way from the senses block.

Thus we advance our model to Figure 11.

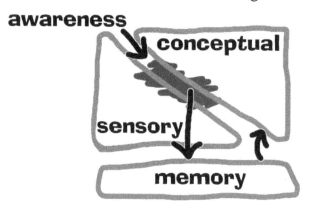

Figure 11. Making the concept block dynamic.

In Figure 11 we think of concept processing as fundamentally different from sensory processing; concept processing is dynamic and creative; it is a sandbox for toying with the memories of objects that have been experienced in the past. By contrast sensory processing is a conveyor belt for data, and any memory that it uses is static and hard-wired and likely embedded into its processing (e.g. for shape, pattern/texture, and motion detection, etc.).

---

5          It also starts to look question-begging: would the puppet-master need a homunculus to operate it? i.e. a separate functioning brain to make sense of the signals it picks up from its puppet strings.

So we are looking at two kinds of brain process (sensory and conceptual) and two kinds of memory (process memory[6] and object memory[7]).

But if we accept the existence of separate object memory, and now introduce Factors #1 and #2 above, how are we able both to write to that memory as well as read from it?

Not only can signals only flow one way through the network of connected dendrites (and would that one-way flow be for reading from, or writing to, memory?) but also if the essence of stored memories is in the arrangement (pattern or topology) of a network of dendrites, how can we incorporate such networks, wholesale, into our concept block?

Should our concept block be massively connected (hard-wired) to the memory block and simply incorporate any memory cluster into its own 'wiring', diverting the inputs and outputs of the cluster into some dynamic process, as and when the concept block calls for it? Indeed, once again we might envisage a puppet-master whose strings, this time, attach to the whole of memory, cluster by cluster, from the concept block (Figure 12).

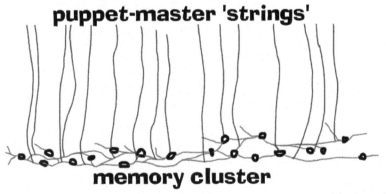

Figure 12. Puppet-master approach between the concept block and the memory block.

---

6        Edges, lines, corners, motion, and possibly more complex shapes.
7        Cats, dogs, cars, faces, characteristic gestures, and events.

Or should we be thinking of somehow copying a whole cluster from the memory block, preserving its patterns of connections (topologies), and recreating the cluster, dynamically, as and where we want it inside the concept block?

If we adopt either a puppet-master approach (borrowing a memory cluster, temporarily wiring it into the concept block) or a cookie-cutter approach (copy a memory cluster wholesale into the concept block), we might usefully redraw our block view with the concept block adjacent the memory block, Figure 13:

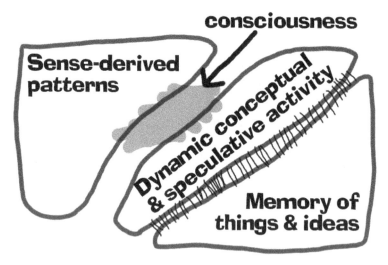

Figure 13. Densely connected concept block and memory block.

Note however that in Figure 13 object memory (of things and ideas) connects only to the concept block.

When the brain is active, we allow concept processing to connect or copy (i.e. load) any part of object memory into the concept processing block to instantiate a dynamic counterpart of that memory, and we allow the focus of processing to move through the sense-derived region, and where the two best match, we posit that attention is focused and consciousness of the matching content arises (as per our model from MIMH).

One simplification that Nature might employ might be to have the same process used for both the concept-to-sensory interaction and for the concept-to-memory interaction.

If this is so, then logically we must allow that any such interaction could generate consciousness (which is what we might expect: we can both recall memories and observe the world) while suggesting at the same time that both local sensory-process memory (for pattern recognition) and object memory (for long term storage) use a similar mechanism for representing data (which we seem to have assumed involves the topology of neural connectivity)[8].

Our diagram might better be Figure 14.

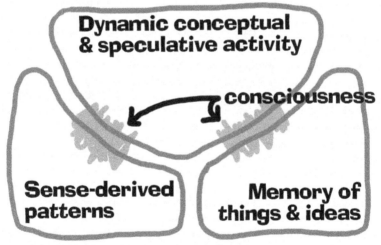

Figure 14. Consciousness can arise from more than one brain activity.

Above, we have casually assumed that we simply pick sensory patterns and memories (both being captured as webs of neural connectivity) and then create a dynamic copy of them in the concept block.

---

8       Remember, this is all conjecture. We are after a brain-ish model, and using Occam's Razor and homunculus avoidance to drive our inquiry, while keeping hold of the conscious element.

**Topology - the pattern of connectivity between neurons**

*(Each neuron in a cluster will show many times this complexity)*

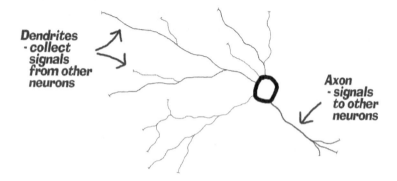

**Dendrites**
*- collect*
*signals*
*from other*
*neurons*

**Axon**
*- signals*
*to other*
*neurons*

Figure 15. The topologies of clusters of neurons will not be easily captured or reproduced.

But how? The topologies, the patterns of connectivity between neurons, are not simple things to either capture or spontaneously reproduce (Figure 15).

So the alternative would be to re-use memories in situ, inside the memory block, and simply wire up the part of the memory block that is wanted, puppet-master style.

There is however a compelling reason for favouring the make-a-copy approach.

Suppose I imagine (or see) a flock of sheep in a field. I can hardly use the puppet-master to connect some untold number of times to the one instance of a sheep I have in memory. Surely I can only see the flock by copying my sheep memory multiple times from memory into the concept block[9].

It would seem that I am going to have to face the

---

9      Although it would seem that, when copying, I can copy more or less of the impression of a sheep and still know it to be a sheep. But I expect to look into that aspect of memory (vagueness, level of detail and so on) later. Besides which, it may be more efficient to replicate the first sheep copy within the concept block, but that would be more an engineering decision for when it comes to implementation.

task of copying a greater or lesser part of the connection topology of some region of neurons from memory into the concept block.

This sounds difficult i.e. reproducing multi-dimensional topologies on demand for temporary use inside the concept block, before re-using that same region of the concept block for something else.

Before I spend time thinking about how I might do it, I find myself asking two questions: (i) How is data actually encoded in these memories? and (ii) How is any one, individual memory found?

For (i): Does the essence of a memory reside in the connectivity of the neurons that constitute it, or does the essence of a memory reside in the external connections between the neurons of this memory and all other memories?

Indeed, do the neurons and their connectivity even matter?—Perhaps all that matters is the output signal from a thus-and-such cluster of neurons, and the output signal happens to be determined by the topology of the connections. Meaning: the topology is a means to an end, not the end in itself.

Well, possibly.

For (ii): How is an individual memory identified and located for any access of any kind?

Surely we are not thinking of an index, like a telephone directory, where people are identified and located from their numerical IDs? How would you find the numerical ID unless you already had the name?[10]

Can we envisage making use of the intrinsic connections (associations) between memories that give each memory its context and its wider meaning?

---

10      Put another way: what's the use of a dictionary to check the spelling of a word, when you don't know how to spell the word in the first place?

If memories are by their nature always associated with one another, we can use these associations to access the memories without adding or inventing a new mechanism (Here we rely on a naive guess that context might reasonably be defined as: a set of associations).

Relying on associations also neatly solves the problem of unique memories. *There is only one Sun* and if you wanted to point to Alpha Centauri instead, you'd use an entirely different set of clues. But clues are all you ever need.

In the next chapter I start to look at ways we might store and retrieve memory data, and hope that some aspect of how storage and retrieval *must* work sheds light on what content and access *must* be like.


Meanwhile (and for a long time now), while the goat has managed to climb into the tree [Figure 8], and has unbusied itself soaking up the heat of the one and only Sun, has it given any thought as to how it will get down, back to ground level, having destroyed the vehicle that gave it a leg up?

# 4. Connectivity and Association

Close to the end of the movie Blade Runner (1982, Dir. Ridley Scott) the android leader Roy Batty (Rutger Hauer) is hunting down the main character Rick Deckard (Harrison Ford) in the Bradbury Building. It's raining outside and the place is dark and empty. The rooms drip with damp; they are echoey and claustrophobic. The camera jumps between Batty's and Deckard's points of view as we see Batty close in on Deckard, who is running scared, and only just keeping ahead through the maze of the building, never sure where the other is...

There is a moment when Batty rams his head all the way through a tiled wall into the room where Deckard is catching his breath. With his head protruding through the wall, Batty eyes the inside of the room...

Naturally the next thing we expect to see is what Batty sees, which is going to be Deckard, and we expect to see the look on Deckard's face—a reaction shot, to let us know just how bad the situation is.

But suppose, the instant Batty has rammed his head through the wall there is a power cut in the cinema (or at home if you're viewing the movie at home) and for all of one minute you are plunged into pitch darkness, and silence.

The last thing you saw or heard was Batty with his head poking through the wall.

One minute later, mains power returns and magically the movie picks up from where it left off, without the slightest glitch.

Now you see Deckard's face, you see his expression—

you see what Batty sees—and you hear Batty's voice challenging Deckard to *do better*.

The point being: when the movie restarts you already have the context of the scene in your mind. You are in the Bradbury building. It's dark, echoey and wet. There is a chase in progress and both you and Batty expect to see Deckard.

All that you need to make sense of what you see on the screen when power returns is context, and you remember the context from the last thing you saw before the power failed.

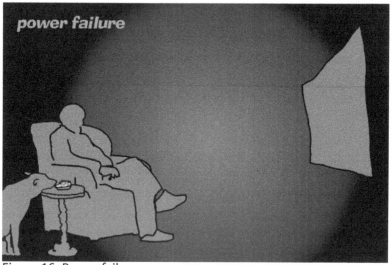

Figure 16. Power failure.

Now let us consider a simple creature that we might suppose is conscious[1].

A bird, a robin say, wakes from sleep and opens its eyes. It sees the side of its nest and surrounding leaves, and possibly trees, and it feels the wind ruffle its feathers.

---

1       I make my supposition given that (a) having consciousness would give it evolutionary advantage, and (b) the kind of processing its brain needs to do, plausibly, requires in some sense the creating of a world view, so that it can be an actor in that world.

At this point, at the moment of waking, its senses feed its brain and it recognises where it is.

Its initial start-up process (call it the bootstrap process if you will) requires its brain to pick out patterns and shapes from the signals coming from its senses and find matching patterns and shapes in memory that correspond to supposed things and stuffs[2] in the physical world[3]. Result: it gains a sense of its place in the world. It is as ready as it possibly can be for whatever happens next.

It is hungry. Hunger prompts the thought of seeds (or other food) and it finds itself motivated to leave the nest, to fly to a location which now comes to mind, where it has found seeds in the past (maybe a bird-feeder that is regularly replenished).

We have endowed this bird with the power to (i) use the information it receives from its senses to assemble a view of the physical world, made meaningful via its memories, and (ii) to anticipate where food may be found in order to satisfy its hunger.

We can probably do away with the apparent sophistication of (ii), anticipation, by treating anticipation as a simple ongoing memory. The bird's memory supplies it with a view of the way its wider world currently is, and it continues to hold this view of the wider world until the world isn't like that any more. This is of course why all memory must be malleable. Memory did not evolve to serve as some absolute historical record. When the world is observed to have changed, so also memory must be changed, to stay up to date. Memory evolved to give its owner a best guess as to what the wider world is currently like[4].

---

2    Some philosophers might elaborate 'things and stuffs' as medium sized white goods [things] and water, wine and cooking oil [stuffs]. Things can be individuated; stuffs are divisible while remaining the same stuff.
3    Presumably the patterns and shapes are processed in some way which allows for variations in orientation, distance and movement.
4    True enough, memories of painful past events are about the past,

With regard to (i) recognition, we have already suggested that memory content is very likely searched for via associations[5], we now have to think of searching for memories via their content[6]—or some mix of the two[7].

In our model we envisage all this time-of-waking activity as taking place in a (perhaps for a robin rather limited) concept block. The robin needs a concept block because if it is only capable of making associations between the sensory block and the memory block, it has no mechanism for accommodating apparently continuously varying object sizes, and relative positions, e.g. as it flies between trees and up to the bird feeder, while avoiding collision with other birds.

Which is to say (for those who might claim a similar case can be made for bees—on which subject I shall remain agnostic), that while some creatures may be able to turn their heads to track their prey before striking (e.g. a barn owl[8]), and others may be hard-wired to a simple fight or flight reaction in response to some shape or shadow or disturbance in their visual field (maybe, a fruit fly[9]), any creature that can distinguish another species and attribute species-specific behaviours to that other species must be in some sense playing out those different behaviours in a concept block.

---

but when the memory is triggered it essentially serves as a present-day warning.

5          Including 'context' which we have suggested is equivalent to a 'set of associations'.

6          Full or partial content; we might search successfully given only fragments.

7          Also, we can assist ourselves (and the robin) if we introduce a mechanism for automatically re-establishing the last context laid down before going to sleep. This would provide a context for the search for things and stuffs, and speed that search up. That way the robin also establishes its world view more quickly (which is good for survival).

8          A barn owl has 437,000,000 neurons in forebrain (source: wikipedia).

9          A fruit fly has 2500 neurons in forebrain (source: wikipedia)—as an indicator of relative sophistication.

In what I have described so far, I rely on being able to access memory in three apparently different ways: to find patterns, to follow associations, and to locate specific memories via context.

But these three are not so different and with a little ingenuity we can reduce all three to a single mechanism, which is association. We can consider context as a set of associations e.g. between some active content in the concept block[10] and memory. And we can consider patterns in terms of the associations e.g. between lesser shapes, sounds, tastes etc. and those more complex compound shapes formed out of the lesser shapes.

We will hold in reserve, for possible use later, the idea that upon waking the concept block assumes the world-context of the most recently laid down memory[11].

How do we propose to use our clusters of memory anyway? How does the neural connectivity mechanism actually work?

When artificial neural networks are trained, the connections between neurons end up being assigned weights (e.g. between 0 and 1[12]) which enable the network as a whole to manipulate input signals to some particular purpose, e.g. to distinguish between images of dogs and cats. The output from such a network might for instance be a single signal bearing a probability value between 0 and 1 (0 it's a dog, 1 it's a cat, 0.5 if it could be either, or neither).

---

10    A viable context might not be the set of *all* associations that lead to a particular object, stuff, place, or time. We only need some subset of all its associations that is sufficient to identify and individuate it in the memory block of a particular individual.

11    For which we would have to propose a mechanism. E.g. assigning different strengths to different associations, or using the number of associations to indicate strength—strength via connectedness. And by allowing more recently established associations to be stronger, for instance by having any associations in any case decay [in strength/number or in speed of response] over time. I.e. when not 'exercised'.

12    A connection weighting of zero effectively turns a connection off.

Suppose one were to replay the outcome from a network like this into a new network, the new network would not know whether it got its input from another neural network (in the memory block or in the sensory block) or from a pocket audio-recorder (to be crude about it).

Previously we have suggested a puppet-master approach where we hijack the inputs and outputs of a neural cluster in memory and, as it were, run the cluster remotely. But perhaps all we need do is to tap the output and activate the memory (by sending a signal to its associative address) and rely on whatever other associations are currently active throughout the memory block to determine the strength and timing of any response the cluster might issue.

This tap-the-output approach would have the benefit of keeping the cluster with all its original associative connections. We would not have to work out or decide how much of the cluster either to hijack (full puppet-master) or copy (cookie-cutter) with the additional worry for the latter of deciding which of the original associative connections must be re-asserted in the new copy.

An assumption all along has been that we can isolate and borrow or use portions of particular individual memories. But if memory is a monolithic interconnected system, how can that be possible?

For the time being, let us continue with what we might think of as a memory cluster, of a size yet to be determined, and possibly of a size determined merely by the complexity of the information it encapsulates.

We have raised three possible methods for incorporating a memory cluster into the concept block: rewire (full puppet-master); borrow output (limited puppet-master); copy connectivity wholesale and reproduce (cookie-cutter).

Each requires a different kind of house-keeping in the concept block.

Our main objection to both puppet-master approaches is that it is not obvious how to contemplate more than one instance of a remembered object at one time. Our main objection to the copy-and-paste approach is not merely how would you achieve the mechanics of it, but how would you reproduce all the associations you would need in order to provide the memory-derived object with its full context of meaning?

(Note that multiple use of a single memory element is a theoretical problem; the mechanics of copying one or more topologies is a practical problem.)

It is worth pausing to think here that we may be conflating at least two kinds of neuron-to-neuron connection. Some connections may be weightings, as are needed for pattern recognition[13]; some may be associations, as will be needed to provide context.

Because of the seemingly intractable problem of multiple instances in the puppet-master strategies, let us see how far we can get with the cookie-cutter approach, and worry about the logistics of it as and when we are forced to.

Suppose that we want to copy the memory of an apple into the concept block.

First we have to locate our memory or memories of an apple. How do we conduct our search?

There would seem to be a number of different options. We could search by name—the sound of the word 'apple', or the shape of the letters in the word 'apple', because surely both of these artefacts from the physical world have some representation in memory, and those representations must be linked (associated) with other aspects of *apple* also maintained in memory.

Or we could search by shape and colour: round and reddish, greenish, yellowish—pick your variety... or there's taste.

---

13      At least in artificial neural networks.

In practice, if consciousness is riding the ribbon of attention (so to speak) something already in consciousness, i.e. some neural arrangement already within the active area of the concept block, will 'throw out' or 'demand' or 'provide' an associative link into memory which the focus of attention will simply follow[14] and will lead to 'apple' memories simply because 'apple' is on our mind.

What does (could) 'follow' mean? Maybe we send a signal down a neural link, a dendrite. What then?

Let's take a step back and look where we are going with this. We have suggested that the concept block must be reconstructive; we will construct discreet, dynamic assemblies of individual memories in the concept block, and somehow 'glue' them together. But these individual memories perhaps themselves each consist of a massively interconnected cluster of neurons. We could be dealing with huge topologies that have to be captured and reproduced. How could we hope to copy any such thing?

The answer has to be a 'serialisation encoding and decoding strategy for topologies' and the 'right kind of neuron' to play the serialisation back on.

Which is to say, we must be able to encode an arbitrarily large connective network into a signal that we can send down an individual dendrite or axon. And we must be able to use that same signal to program the connectivity of some flexibly connectible neurons in the concept block.

Suppose, then, that we can request that a memory cluster sends us its serialised connectivity map. Do we do this by sending a request signal to a specific memory, and how do we receive the serialisation code in return (i.e. how do we know where to connect to for 'output'?)

What we really need (thinking like an engineer or programmer) is to be able to send a request into some

---

14      We do not invent the presence of an apple out of the blue. Even the surrealists (professionals at odd juxtapositions) had to invent games in order to generate apparently random, spontaneous 'ideas' that they could or would not arrive at 'naturally' via chains of either associative or rational thought.

standard request input port in the memory block and wait for a result to emerge from some standard output port. We would then be *decoupling* the memory block from the concept block, and relying only on a single connection[15]. Instead of associative neural links, we would have an encoded address signal.

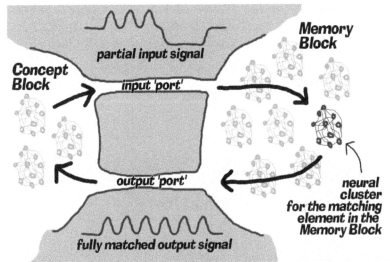

Figure 17. The Memory Block with input and output ports.
An incomplete pattern might be sent to the input port, and broadcast throughout the Memory Block. The partial address pattern is enough of an address to locate the full memory (or element) and the complete memory pattern is then published through the output port.

In fact, if we had a serialisation algorithm for connectivities/topologies, we could use the serial signal produced by the algorithm to 'address' a particular memory cluster. If we sent the encoded address signal into the memory block input port, the signal would be distributed throughout memory, but only the memory cluster with the matching address would respond and

15    Which might be quite high bandwidth and with built-in redundancy against deterioration through physical trauma or aging, so it would not be a single axon, indeed could be many thousands.

issue, for instance, the serialisation sequence that characterises the content of that memory[16], Figure 17.

In the next chapter I propose a serialization scheme and cluster (re-)construction scheme.

For now, let us revisit our block diagram from the last chapter, Figure 14.

We can shrink the concept block from a region where a wide range of concepts, from high level to low, are processed into a much slimmer highly dynamic sandbox where, also, consciousness is possible, Figure 18.

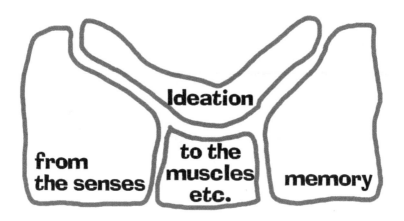

Figure 18. Ideation plus motor activities (which we locate partway between memory, which can be read and written, and data from the senses, which can only be read).

---

16      We are assuming that the encoded connectivity *content* of a memory cluster requires considerably longer serialization sequences than are needed to *address* the cluster. Otherwise we might as well use the content sequence to address the cluster, at which point it feels like something has gone wrong: why would we use the sequence to query the cluster to deliver the sequence we already have? But it might make supreme good sense because (i) when we are pattern-matching our sequence (our pattern) may be incomplete, and because (ii) ultimately what we are after is the whole panoply of other memories *associated with* the memory [cluster] for which we have an address, and these could be tagged onto the end of the published serialized address.

I now rename the concept block *Ideation*, because the block is no longer thought of as dealing only with high level concepts, but also can help itself to the more directly perceived objects of the sensory block.

Figure 18 presents at block level how the Lock Step tray model might be realized, both in real brains and in machine brains. This is not to claim this is how brains are organized; it is to claim that any brain organized like this, in this understandable way, could become functionally equivalent to a real brain of similar functional capacity. It is also to say that were this model instantiated as a machine, unless consciousness is deliberately introduced (i.e. via a gleeon-datum mating mechanism) the machine would not be conscious and would lack the 'edge' that consciousness brings with it (MIMH Chapter 7).


In the movie Blade Runner, when the android Roy Batty (Rutger Hauer) pokes his head through the wall and opens his eyes, does he see what we would see in the same circumstances? (aside from flashing lights and stars from impact of head on wall)

As a model *Nexus-6* replicant (android), Batty has only had a few years to learn everything he needs to learn about the world. Indeed, in the Blade Runner universe the designer of the *Nexus-6*, Eldon Tyrell (Joe Turkel), was so concerned that in time the *Nexus-6* would develop emotions that he gave the *Nexus-6* models a limited life span.

Batty presumably lacks the rich hinterland of nuance and meaning that a human would normally have picked up by the time they reached adulthood.

What memories does Batty draw upon?

Does he see and understand Deckard (Harrison Ford)

in the same terms as he (Batty) sees himself[17]? I.e. that 'humans are just like us replicants, only they live longer.'

Is not any mentally less richly endowed creature bound to think of any mentally more richly endowed creature as a version of itself, i.e. not see any added sophistication? Necessarily, the lesser sees through the filter of its own impoverished outlook (Or, importantly, reversing the argument: *there is a risk to humans that we might only understand any AI as a version of ourselves and grossly underestimate it*—although we are smart enough to recognise that as a risk. In principle. But what then?).

So how could Batty read more into this other creature than he (Batty) had himself experienced?

---

17      A conceit of the movie, via the unicorn flashback and origami figure, is the question of whether Deckard himself is an android. And yet if Deckard knows the content of Rachael's false memories, why should not Gaff (Edward James Olmos), who makes the origami figures, not know what (the human) Deckard's fantastical dreams are like, for instance if Deckard's memories had previously been collected in order to be gifted to an android at some point in the future?

## 5. Serialization Rights

I once found myself lying on a gurney in a hospital, unable to move and with my neck clamped.

A rogue driver had jumped his turn at a mini roundabout and rammed me. By the time the doctors had completed their tests and found me a bed it was late, and dark outside, and when I was wheeled into the ward, the main lights were off.

I had no idea where I was. My only view of the world was of the ceiling where I caught the occasional scattered or reflected light from some instrument or other. The dominant feature of this nightscape was the incessant beeping of monitors. Each seemed possessed by its own signature tone and, as the night wore on, with intermittent alarms that would summon a nurse (I guessed it was a nurse who responded because I couldn't move, or see anything). The nurse could be heard to perform some checks, perhaps whisper some kind words, and then depart through swing doors—I knew they were swing doors because I heard them swing.

From all these sounds, plus the hazy impression of the distance I travelled as I was wheeled into the ward, I built up some idea of the room, its size and shape, and the location of beds.

In my mind's eye, I figured there were probably twenty beds, and the ward itself I estimated was about the size of a small car park.

Even when it grew light, and I could make out at least the ceiling and light fittings above me, I had to keep guessing about the size and shape of the area, and all the evidence was that my estimation from the night before was about right.

But when eventually I was allowed to sit up: *How wrong could I be!*

Why do I recall this now? Because there is an assumption that lurks in the shadows of our investigation that so far remains unvoiced. It is this:

We seem to be working towards the assumed goal that reproducing what we perceive—the sum of all qualia[1] as they exist from moment to moment—is all that is required for a brain to function cognitively.

Put another way, our assumption is that if we can reproduce the cinema screen of our conscious experience and paint pictures on it—as if firing up pixels on a screen—then just by so doing, even without consciousness, we have reproduced a functional (and functioning) brain-like apparatus.

This, of course, cannot be true. Otherwise Nature would simply have placed a qualia-producing mechanism across the retina at the back of the eye. And why would that not work? Because the patterns of light so detected would have no meaning.

Which is to say, the brain must deliver meaning to the mind[2].

There must be a whole lot going on behind the scenes in a real brain for which merely 'plausibly recreating' the experience does not deliver functional equivalence.

That said, by exploring a setup which at least looks like it will deliver the range and content we are after must at least be a good starting point. And let us, now, be open to the possibility of including meaning if we come across

---

1      A quale is a single sensation: a patch of colour, a sound, a taste, a smell, etc. The plural of quale is qualia. See also MIMH Chapter 6.
2      And meaning, surely, is something that only comes with consciousness. Whether or not a pseudo-conscious machine can operate cognitively without incorporating fully conscious, capital M, *Meaning* remains to be seen.

a good candidate to deliver it.

With that in mind, and in terms of Ideation in our building block model, and having chosen to try to get the model to work using a memory cluster re-creation mechanism, what we need is a way to encode neural connectivity into a serial stream (and decode a serial stream back into neural connectivity).

If we can master encoding and decoding we should be able to make temporary copies of neuronal clusters inside Ideation. The temporary copies can then be manipulated dynamically in what will amount to active thought processes—that, at least, is the current, working idea.

A side benefit of having connectivity-to-serial encoding, and the corresponding decoding, is that we will be able to search memory simply by injecting a serial signal and waiting for what we might think of as a 'resonance' pattern match in response[3].

The question is: how does one map a brain-cell topology into a serial signal (and then reconstitute the topology, dynamically inside Ideation)?

An initial idea might be to inject a strong pulsed signal into a dendrite and look for reflections and echoes wherever the signal encounters a branch or is connected to another neuron. Then some kind of signal processing[4] would be performed on the pattern of signal reflections, as one might with the echoes produced by banging a hammer at the mouth of a complex of caves; delay times and amplitude might, if the rules for signal attenuation are known, be used to infer the structure, or topology, of the cave system.

---

3    The same serial signal might be used both to encode cluster content (topologies) and to address the cluster (through the memory input port), or, different serial signals might be used for addresses and for the topologies. However we use any encoding/decoding system, simply having such a system opens up opportunities.
4    A bit like radar.

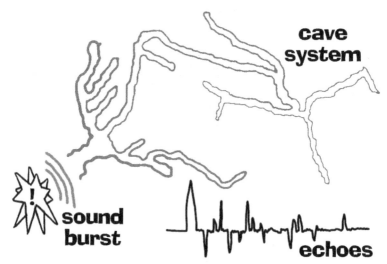

Figure 19. Echoes might be used to work out the topology of the cave system.

However, this scheme involves a good deal of signal processing, and do we ever observe signals of this kind in dendrites? In addition to which: would it always work, for are there not different topological configurations which would give rise to exactly the same response signal and thus be indistinguishable from one another?

The answer I propose (which may or may not be how a real brain does things; all I need is a plausible approach that the brain might take which I could adapt to work for an artificial thinking machine) is to treat the topology of a dendrite as a maze. The signal I generate will be a record of my decisions as I navigate the maze. I hope to arrive at a simple binary signal that describes the topology of one complete dendritic [tree] structure, as follows:

Suppose I think of the dendrite topology as consisting of forks and terminuses, and treating the topology as a maze, suppose I offer a recipe to navigate the maze as: *Explore Every Fork*.

From the base of the dendrite (where it emerges from the body [soma] of the neuron) I 'walk' until I meet the first fork. This most likely will be a simple two-way junction, but could be three-way or more, which is fine.

At this first fork I arbitrarily choose one branch. I record my decision to take a branch by writing 'F' in my notepad. I follow the branch. Suppose it terminates without further branching at the synapse of another neuron. Now I mark 'T' in my notepad. I retrace my steps back to the fork and take the next branch (suppose there were actually three branches, for the sake of illustration). I add another 'F' to my notepad. I follow this branch and come to a fork. I arbitrarily select a branch, take it and record 'F' in my notepad. It terminates: 'T', then 'F' for the next branch, and so on.

From trial and error, I discover this method doesn't quite work, because I can't tell when I have completed exploring a branch. So I will insert an additional 'T' when I retrace my steps and step out of a branch.

I now have a means of capturing the topology of a dendrite as a stream of 'F's and 'T's which I can easily convert to a series of electro-chemical spikes for a real dendrite, or a series of 0s and 1s for a digital computer. (And if I wanted to record the weighting of a particular dendrite branch—should that prove necessary to the model—I can replace the T's with a non-zero number (the weighting) between zero and 1.)

There is a question about how I generate this sequence for any one dendrite tree which for now I will offer a cheat, which is to say: I will ask the neuron cell body, and expect it to be able to tell me.

The next question is: how can I use an FT-list to dynamically[5] reproduce a topology whenever it is wanted inside Ideation?

For this, I borrow from an idea in computer science, which is known as a shift register, or known from

---

5    I.e. so that such an arrangement can be created and deleted at will in any position, and maybe at more than one position at a time, in Ideation.

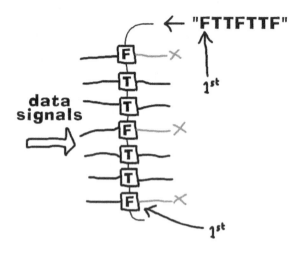

Figure 20: Switch Register.

computer programming as a FIFO (first in first out), plus a little adaptation:

The register (I will call it a Switch Register) is a row of cells, connected like links in a chain, each of which can hold one bit (or unit or value) of data. I can load the serial signal into this register from one end, so that each 'F' and 'T' element in the signal ends up in a cell, preserving the order of the signal, Figure 20.

However in this case, in our Switch Register, each cell operates a simple switch, controlling one line of data. For instance, a 'T' will indicate the switch is 'on' or 'closed' i.e. a signal can pass along the associated line to another neuron. An 'F' will indicate the switch is 'off' or 'open' so that a signal cannot pass along the associated line. If our model needs to support different weightings for different branches in the topology, then we can pass a signal with weighted values between 0 and 1 to the Switch Register, and each switch will only pass some fraction of the signal it receives.

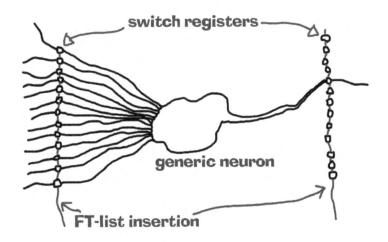

Figure 21. Separate dendrites' inputs are all switched by the content of the Switch Register, which in turn is controlled by the FT-list.

If we now combine the switch register with a generic and massively connected neuron, we can arbitrarily control the connectivity of that neuron to the outside world, Figure 21.

Two possible objections are:

1) The original topology captured by the FT-list is destroyed. We have not reproduced the branches of the original. This is true, but we have reproduced the inter-neuron connectivity. No matter how many terminuses there were in the original (say) memory neuron, we have created the possibility of a connection from this generic neuron to another generic neuron for each of those terminuses. So the overall neuron-to-neuron topology will be preserved.

2) We have lost any processing that occurs inside the dendrite tree that might arise from the relative locations of branches, e.g. any local signal suppression effects (as per recently observed XOR[6] behaviour seen in dendrites

6      XOR stands for 'exclusive OR'. It is a logical operator in the same way that '+' or '-' are mathematical operators. XOR acts on two variables, say

before signals even reach the neuron's cell body). To this, in this iteration of the model, I must plead *mea culpa*. But I do hope that this iteration of the model will provide enough functionality in practice to allow us to say "OK, so far so good, let's now engineer the difference by using some other, smarter encoding."

What we are proposing, however, is that large contiguous clusters of neurons are copied from memory in this way. Indeed we might think in terms of a sufficient number of neurons to produce a single quale, which (as per MIMH chapter 6) may mean numbers in their thousands[7].

There remains a question about what happens along the boundary of a cluster of neurons copied into Ideation in this scheme. Thinking in terms of pixels on a computer screen, what kind of connections does one Ideation cluster (delivering, say, a patch of yellow) have with another (say, delivering a patch of green).

Part of the answer might be to suggest that Ideation has a granularity: the smallest quale has a certain size of say (picking a random number for the sake of illustration) 1000 neurons. This would be the capacity of each cluster in Ideation, and a neural framework, or infrastructure, would enclose each cluster of 1000 generic neurons and

---

'A' and 'B', in the same way that '+' acts on two variables, say 'p' and 'q'. p + q = something-or-other. A XOR B = something-or-other. For '+' the rule is addition. For XOR the rule is the logic of 'exclusive OR'. The XOR operator is a variation on the OR operator. The outcome of a logic operator is either 'True' or 'False' (sometimes T or F, sometimes represented by 1 or 0). The outcome of A OR B is True if either A is True or B is True or both are True. The outcome of A XOR B is True if either A is True or B is True but not both are True. The 'X' in XOR is for exclusive: One variable being True must exclude the other being True.

7          There may be an issue with the time a long serially encoded signal takes to complete its journey between memory and Ideation i.e. load time, but let's see if we can get to a viable model before worrying about optimizations.

manage all inter-cluster house-keeping activity (yet to be defined).

In terms of consciousness (thinking in terms of the Lock Step/gleeon model of MIMH) the gleeons do not have to be continuous and adjacent, they merely have to be close enough to provide a continuum of resonance in the gleeon field. Consciousness could be patchily generated across the brain while still experienced as a continuous, seamless whole.

Indeed this kind of patchy consciousness inside Ideation may be necessary, since when a mind anticipates the motion of mechanical objects (a tennis ball is dropped and we expect it to bounce) the process of anticipation— the calculation itself—is not part of what we perceive. We only perceive, in our mind's eye, an expected location (and move our hand accordingly, to drive the racket into the ball).

We make no attempt here to propose the relative locations of the qualia-producing, the estimation (calculation), and the visualisation (speculation) clusters in Ideation. Although according to the Ideation model so far, we might suppose we could position any of them anywhere within Ideation 'space' so long as the qualia-producing clusters sit in a spatial arrangement that accords with the continuities we experience: object A is left of object B, which is below object C, and so on.

The fact that we are going to have to include[8] the ability to navigate the world in the search for food, and anticipate the behaviour of prey and mates, means we need to have a way of incorporating *behaviours*[9] into our memory model, and associate those behaviours with items in memory, and to bring those behaviours out of memory just like their qualia-bearing counterparts.

---

8     Part of an evolutionary necessity and motivation for having a brain.
9     The estimation (calculation) and visualization (speculation) components, above.

Indeed, perhaps behaviour memories should be entirely separate from those qualia-bearing object-based counterparts: can one not imagine in one's mind's eye, 'a brick bouncing like a tennis ball' or 'a tortoise leaping like a tiger'. Strangely surreal combinations can be brought to mind without difficulty, suggesting behaviours are more like memory clusters in their own right, linked to the memory of an object by association rather than constitutive of the memory of that particular physical object.


In the next chapter I will explore ways in which Ideation and Memory might work together, with a view to refining and revising the raw ideas presented in this chapter.

As for the hospital ward, it was the size of a small restaurant. There were six beds and one nurse, who sat at a table and was on duty, and present, always, all night. My bed was next to the main window and the swing doors I had been listening to could have been any of half a dozen sets of door that led off the corridor at the far end of the ward. I could hear beeps and alarms from the adjacent wards and the soundscape I had invented included places that did not exist—being on the far side of brick walls, outside the building itself. When I sat up in bed I occupied an entirely different world from the one I had pictured, unseen.

# 6. Tip of the Tongue Moments

*Who was that actor that was in that movie Thingy you know the one, and you know, that other movie, Doodah? Whatsaname, you know who I mean...*

How can you recall something from memory when you don't know what it is?

*You know, she played Martha, wife of a history professor in that Mike Nichols film...*

We usually have clues, of course, but even so, sooner or later, there is always that 'Something I had to do as soon as I got home but now I'm back I can't remember.'

*She married the husband in real life, too. Several times, in fact. You must remember Whatsaname forchrissakes?*

Recognizing objects, or situations, or answering a question from just one clue might well be achieved through the use of associations between neurons (or between clusters of neurons) but what do we think the mechanism is, in practice?

In this text so far, we have mooted the possible use of FT-lists to query and extract the topologies of memory clusters, but even then, how do FT-lists fit into the larger picture and help us get the work of our thought-experimental brain done?

In the Lock Step model the ribbon of consciousness is forever moving, following what seems to be of most interest one moment to the next. We take focus of attention to be where there is most activity. We posit that this focus moves to maximize meaning, which for us means to seek out the most significant aspects (associations) of whatever currently is in focus.

The ribbon of attention moves by either pursuing associations that are attached to the current focus of attention or by being drawn to some new experience which arrives from the senses.

In this way, once consciousness is established, it is self-driving and only ever has to chase associations to keep going. The machinery never stops.

The initial boot-up process is slightly different. On arousal after any loss of consciousness Ideation fetches the most recent stored context from memory. It matches the currently available sensory data to this context and thereafter all activity is based on following associative links.

We have presented a model of how Ideation might replicate memory clusters, but we have not addressed the question of how the associative links from those memory clusters are made available to the copies in Ideation. I.e. how are associative links preserved inside Ideation for use when chasing down the next thing to copy and paste from memory?

As it happens, we have a ready-made mechanism to hand.

So far we have thought about two types of neuron-to-neuron connection (i) a (possibly weighted) connectivity/topology link inside a memory cluster, and (ii) an association from one memory cluster to another.

We need a way to preserve any associative links from a neural cluster that we have copy-pasted into Ideation so that those links still lead to the original associated

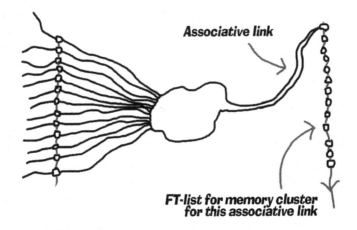

**Associative link**

**FT-list for memory cluster
for this associative link**

**When the associative link fires, the FT-list is broadcast**

Figure 22. To implement an associative link, we re-purpose the switch register.

cluster in Memory. What we can do is connect the as yet unreferenced associative link from the Ideation copy of the neuron to a Switch Register that contains the FT-list for the address of the associated cluster[1], Figure 22.

Given the ability to encode and decode an FT-list, how are we going to connect Ideation and Memory?

As suggested in 4. Connectivity and Association we can decouple Ideation from Memory by sending FT-list address requests to Memory via a request input 'port', and receiving FT-list responses from Memory via an output 'port' where the input ports are specialist (dedicated) dendrites and the output ports are specialist (dedicated) axons.

In order to pursue an association from a copy of a memory cluster that currently resides in Ideation we have only to direct the FT-list for that association into an

---

1      We can stipulate a simple rule of the architecture (technology or implementation) that when a Switch Register is used to store an associative link, it adopts some special mode or operating state so that it issues its FT-list contents to the memory input port when it is triggered by the one axon that connects to it.

input port, and wait for a response from an output port. Both ports can be conceived of as serving the same locale[2] in the Ideation substrate.

That may give us a mechanism for retaining simple associative connections inside Ideation, but what of contexts and patterns which are each implemented as a set of associative links?

First a digression. Let us think about the boot-up process.

Our starting point for boot-up is to request the most recently remembered context from memory.

A simple mechanism specifically for 'last remembered context' might be a set of Switch Registers that are continually updated with important associations[3] when those associations are loaded into Ideation. If Ideation becomes inactive (unconsciousness) then loading the clusters identified here, as consciousness is recovered, quickly restores the most likely true, real-world context of the creature into Ideation.

But what would count as the start-up context?

The robin is in its nest.

The patient is in bed in hospital.

We could do worse than suppose that the most important aspects of start-up context are the tangible indicators of location, and the tangible indicators of location are likely to be common to all the clusters (recognised objects) currently loaded into Ideation. So context would be the set of associative links that occur in the greatest number among those clusters currently in Ideation.

At boot-up we: (a) fetch the links for the last remembered context from our special last-known-

---

2          I use the word 'locale' because I expect there to be more than one pair of memory ports. At least for the moment I want to raise the possibility that there are different ports for, at least, different sense-based data, audio and visual etc.

3          As represented by their FT-lists.

context memory[4], and (b) search memory for patterns that are currently manifest in the sensory block, given the newly remembered context.

Our search generates a series of FT-lists of the best matching objects in memory and these lists now appear at the output port[5].

The FT-lists are used to re-create memory clusters in Ideation, in places across Ideation that correspond to their relative positions in, for instance, the visual field in the senses block.

We have suggested how a single associative link might pick out (or locate) a single memory cluster, but how would a pattern?

A pattern may be either the single FT-list to a well-known shape (like a hexagon, for a mathematician). Or a pattern may be a set of associative links, where each link references one of several shapes that are constitutive of some more complex shape not encountered before.

In common with FT-lists for context that are sent to the memory input port, unfamiliar patterns involve a series of FT-lists. How does memory respond to more than one FT-list at a time?

The answer is, we simply submit the list of lists to the memory input port and as each memory cluster is located, and lights up, not only does it publish the FT-list of its internal connectivity, but it also activates all its associative links.

Any memory clusters which are linked to associatively from two or more of the clusters in the context/pattern list will be multiply invoked and consequently publish an

---

4      We might be able to do this without a special last-known-context memory (later in this chapter).

5      In order for FT-lists to be usable this will likely be more sophisticated than a single list. There will probably have to be lists of lists, with some for connectivity, and some for association. But, given the initial FT-list encoding method, it should be no more than any experienced computer programmer might routinely do, to come up with a list consolidation technique.

FT-list (connectivity) with higher priority, or weighting (or whatever mechanism for relative importance we might implement).

We might think of a context list of FT-lists causing a voting storm across memory, and one or two memories will come out on top, and their FT-lists will be published first and most prominently. By the time secondary or tertiary FT-lists are arriving at the output port, likely other memory requests will be taking over, in strength and prominence[6].


In drilling down into the details of how FT-lists might be used, we have gone a long way to offering a functional model. However one question which has not been mentioned yet is that of scale.

We have not touched on how long an FT-list might be (with implications for the internal architecture of Ideation) nor how many neurons might constitute a functional cluster, e.g. that might contribute to a quale [MIMH Chapter 6]. Indeed, most likely we would not want to search for content that matches a single FT-list (i.e. for the dendrite trees of one neuron), but content from numerous interconnected neurons inside a memory cluster together with their collective dendrite topologies (thus in reality we will be using complexes or composites or lists of FT-lists).

If the human brain has some 86 billion neurons and 100 trillion connections, in round numbers that gives us an average of about 1000 connections for each neuron. Using FT-list encoding, and if we were to assume a dendrite could carry distinct electro-chemical spikes of 1mS duration, with 1mS between spikes, it would

---

6      And remembering this is all speculation. We aim to build our own brain-ish machine that plausibly shows us how any machine could entertain concepts. We are not trying to explain how real brains work, which will be steeped in the expediencies of Nature.

take two seconds to convey a full list. So clearly some optimisation must happen, but for the time being let's see if we can prove that the addressing scheme works for the overall model in principle (if slowly), and look at real-life optimisations once an operational architecture has been developed.

For the time being we might arbitrarily think in terms of 1000 neurons for a functional memory block, and arbitrarily think of an average of 300 connections for each, and scale up or down as needed later.

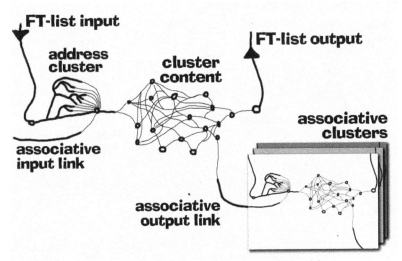

Figure 23. A memory cluster. One FT-list is used to address a memory cluster. Another FT-list is used to represent the topology of its content. The second list is published when the cluster is addressed, either via an associative link, or by matching its FT-list address from the input port.

Let us now consider what a memory cluster might look like.

I will look at two models for a cluster: in the first, the cluster address scheme is independent of connectivity/ topology content (Figure 23).

In the second, I attempt to make the address match the connectivity content, in an attempt to make the memory addressing associative (i.e. so that you could in principle search by content. This may or may not be necessary for the architecture to work, but it strikes me as a useful possibility to explore) Figure 24.

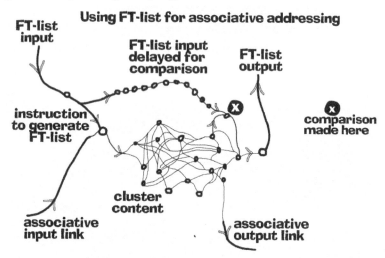

Figure 24. A memory cluster. If the input port FT-list matches the self-generated FT-list then we trigger publication of the self-generated FT-list and activate all the associative links.

In overview our memory clusters are going to serve a number of different kinds of memory and a reasonable starting place might be to think of clusters as belonging to one of various different kinds and varieties:

We have sense-based memories, visual, audio, touch, taste, smell, and many more.

We have behavioural memories, relating to turning, running, dropping, throwing, winking, wagging and so on.

We also have body-state memories, such as fear, joy, anxiety and so on (some of which might actually be thought of as sensory) but also body-clock related memories which crucially, I suggest, play a part in locating initial context when we are aroused to consciousness.

Upon arousal, our body clock is in some state or other (unfelt body chemistry plus e.g. daylight), and that state will key in the expected, remembered context for that 'time of day'. If we wake up in a strange bed we are disorientated and have to re-establish context the hard way by trying to remember what we were doing the night before as well as examining the objects around us and working out from their associations where we might be.

Without for the time being coming down either for or against the fully associative addressing model, one question that arises for either scenario is: How are new memories created?

One might suppose that a new memory starts with a list of associations that are, on repeated occasions, not satisfied. The first thing to be established would have to be the address and input-output framework, devoid of content. Subsequently the connective/topological content would be inserted, or develop (depending on the kind of memory cluster and how its content is encoded).

The question of forming new memories suggests a further address-decoding scheme, Figure 25.

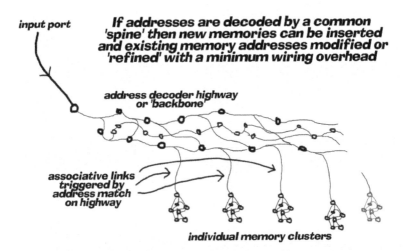

Figure 25. A common spine for decoding addresses might make adding and modifying addresses easier.

However, if part or all of a cluster address is decoded by the spine, we cannot implement associative memory addressing because there would be duplication of data in the spine and in the cluster itself[7].

In order to have spinal decoding *and* associative addressing, the spine would have to be monolithic (i.e. capture all of memory), and the clusters would have to be reduced in size to contain only associative links. Which is to say, the spine would contain the memory content.

This might offer equivalent functionality to the schemes in either Figure 23 or Figure 24; it might boil down to a question of trade-offs during implementation.

The discussion above gives us a handle on what, in broad terms, a memory cluster might look like, and how it might operate. The alternative working structures demonstrate the kinds of ideas and tools and flexibilities available to us to play with in what follows.

And if, all this time, you've been wondering about *Whatsaname*, *Whatsaname* was of course Elizabeth Taylor in "Who's Afraid of Virginia Woolf?" (1966 Dir. Mike Nichols), in which she suffers a similar crisis of memory, trying to conjure up the name of some actress or other...

---

7          This is an absolute rule we impose on our design: *There is only one Sun.*

# 7. Never the Same Sheep Twice

Let us review how our Ideation-based mechanism might operate and see what gaps remain to be filled.

For instance, how would such a system 'boot up' for the first time ever, with nothing in memory? Thereafter, how would it 'boot up' for each successive session of thinking?

Let me look at the second question first, since the Ideation mechanism is conceived of as dynamic and always running, and if I can describe it while it is actively working, I can see what is needed and must be provided, or acquired, to have it boot up to that fully functional state.

Figure 26. A view through a window of a sheep in a field.

## A Sheep in a Field

Let us first run the Ideation-based brain on a simple static scene: You blink your eyes open and discover a view through a window onto an almost empty green field.

Let us suppose that a hedge encloses the field, with a bright red gate and there is one solitary white sheep, and the focus of your attention is on the sheep.

## Re-assembling the Field of View

Signals from the senses (here mainly the eyes) are processed through stages in the sensory block of our model brain to identify a variety of simple shapes and details. Ideation matches[1] complexes of these shapes to objects in memory, using features[2] of the sensed shapes to infer the orientation, lighting etc. that must be applied to the object in memory when the object in memory is copied into Ideation, i.e. to re-construct the best cognitive match for what comes from the senses.

Having matched a sheep shape to the memory of a sheep, Ideation does not merely load what a sheep should look like at that distance, facing that way, in that light, etc. but it also loads the associations that memory provides to accompany the memory of a sheep, as well as loading associations for its current contextual modifiers[3].

Ideation, then, has copied some set of neuron clusters

---

1      Ideation does not have to do all of the matching, of course. Some of the pattern matching is done by memory because memory addressing is associative. Ideation can send a partial pattern to memory and memory can respond with the best-guess match. Which is to say: brains like this can and will make errors as a result of paucities of data or paucities of memories.

2      Texture, perspective-like distortions, etc. including the stuff of visual illusions. Some feature analysis might also be done in the sensory block. But operations like perspective adjustments should only occur in one place. Incoming sensory and recreated [Ideation] objects might receive perspectival twists in Sensory or Memory or Ideation, but only one of these can serve any particular function; duplication of function is no more welcome than duplication of [memory] data.

3      Distance, orientation, lighting etc.

and replicated them locally for its own use. But how are the copies wired together?

A key assumption we are going to rely on is that each Ideation cluster block, when it (a) instantiates sense-based data, and (b) is part of a real physical brain[4], also contributes (some or all of) a quale of sensory experience to what we perceive, and further, that in so doing this quale ends up, *without any further processing*[5], adjacent to the next quale in the cinema screen effect that we behold with our inner eye (our visual impression of the world). Which is to say, the relative arrangement (topology) of adjacent qualia in our perceived field of view must be the same as the topology of adjacent sense-based Ideation clusters.

Similarly, the topology of clusters in Ideation that correspond to processed sensory data must follow the topology of their unprocessed counterparts at the back of the eye. That is: we *require* that the topology of qualia-producing neurons corresponds to the topology of objects as we perceive them in the physical world.

(This is not to say there are not gaps, merely it is to say that qualia for the front right leg of the sheep are not produced from a region in Ideation among qualia which represent two branches of the tree—unless the sheep is up the tree).

(Also it is not to say the location of the metaphorical cinema screen (or ribbon of consciousness as per MIMH) is fixed in some specific area of Ideation[6]; mind has no concept of its own location; the source of the whole collective of qualia could be shifting wildly across the

---

4    When our brain-ish model is implemented in neurons etc. and in a manner that results in consciousness.
5    We cannot allow further processing. Further processing would have to be performed by a homunculus and all homunculean activity must be confined to the physical brain, as per MIMH.
6    Ideation could in principle be located anywhere in the brain, especially if Ideation is intimately integrated with and distributed among other functionality of the brain, across the brain.

**Neural clusters in Ideation**

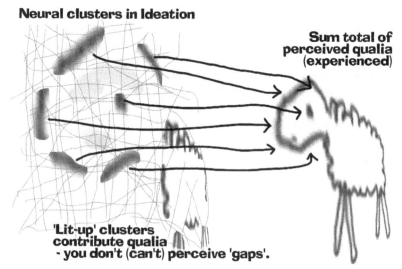

Figure 27. Topology is preserved between qualia-generating clusters in Ideation and the perceived experience (The topology found in the data from the senses is already preserved in the physical relationship between clusters in Ideation).

brain from micro-second to micro-second and not disrupt our experience[7]).

This topological equivalence (qualia to Ideation to retina) may be an outrageously bold suggestion (not to say a hopelessly naive conception of how the brain works— some readers will no doubt be muttering expletives under their breaths) but if we do not allow ourselves this assumption (in fact, we must insist on it) we have to invent a homunculus who can sort out and organize all the available qualia into a coherent, meaningful whole, i.e. to explain why we perceive the world as a single joined-up unified thing—and the arguments in MIMH and its conclusions were driven by the principle that the homunculus must be removed from the scene (or at least stripped of all its clothes, which MIMH achieved, down to the pre-conscious gleeon)[8]. The albeit convenient

---

7        So long as the collective of qualia remains either continuous or spatio-temporally overlapping.
8        The other driver for the inquiry in MIMH being Occam's Razor.

temptation to introduce a homunculus to solve the problem of spatial arrangement is simply not available to us.

"But hold on!" Say you. "This must be wrong! For Nature is economical (precisely why Occam's Razor is so powerful and why you, *Dear Author*, promote it to the $n^{th}$ degree). So would not Nature simply insert gleeon-capture and qualia-production at the back of the eye, across the retina? We would simply focus on a patch of red, and see red, and *End of Story!*"

This is true in that, were Nature to do that, some awareness of some pattern of light would exist somewhere in the universe, but that pattern would mean nothing.

I repeat: The pattern would mean nothing.

Ideation finds and adds meaning to the signals that come from the senses.

We must load more into Ideation than a mere copy of what the sensory block has produced as a result the sensory block's analysis of the sheep-shape into constituent parts[9].

The something 'more' that is loaded into Ideation must contribute to meaning and that meaning must be conveyed to the qualia of our overall experience, *somehow*.

### How Do We Assign Meaning to a Concept?

When I say the words or think of or perceive a sheep in a field, part of what it means for there to be a sheep in a field is for me to understand what is meant by that strange-shaped object, the sheep. With the simple recognition that it is a sheep I can bring to bear all sorts of thoughts and associations related to my rational (and perhaps also irrational, if fearful) beliefs and cogitations,

---

9      At the very least we had to interpret patterns in the sensory data and speculate, as per the Lock Step model, that the thing before us was a sheep, and affirm such things about the extracted patterns e.g. via associations, i.e. to arrive at our understanding that the shape we see is a thing we think of as a sheep.

memories, theories, sensory experiences, associations etc. about sheep. Were I, a second later, to decide it was a snowman, I would instantly (as I perceive it[10]) replace all those thoughts and beliefs with a radically different set of thoughts and beliefs (unless it was a sheep made of snow, with coal for eyes and a cauliflower tail, I guess).

Initially then, I propose to say that the meaning I attach to 'a sheep' is the sum total of all the associated thoughts etc. (as above) that are available to me when I conjure up the image of a sheep in my mind's eye[11], or recognise a sheep in a field.

To *mean* something, the patch of white that is the sheep must be identified as a sheep and we must know what a sheep is like.

Here I think it is useful to introduce a distinction which some philosophers make between what are known as primary and secondary qualities.

Secondary qualities refer to sensations (colour, sound, taste, smell etc.) which we derive from the physical world directly (as it seems) through our senses. Secondary qualities are by their nature subjective—exclusive to the person experiencing them.

Primary qualities refer to characteristics of objects in the physical world such as solidity, motion, extension, shape and number which, while we infer these qualities from their secondary qualities, these primary qualities are rooted in the physical world and can be independently verified and objectively agreed upon.

In this text, so far, we have sought to represent those things in Ideation of which we are conscious, mostly and not unsurprisingly, in terms of their secondary qualities.

In so doing we may inadvertently have excluded one or more classes of property necessary to a proper and

---

10    Possibly punctuated by a brief period of confusion while I examine the grey-white blob for some feature I recognize.
11    The mind's eye view must also be part of Ideation.

complete representation of a thing, for instance, its three-dimensional extension in space.

## Meaning (M) and meaning (m)

We should at least ask: Do we (in some way) perceive primary qualities? i.e. are there qualia that correspond to primary qualities, albeit not delivered to us directly from any of our physical senses (how could they be?), and less prominent in the world we experience than their garish secondary cousins?

Not only do I think we should not rule out the possibility *tout court* but, thinking in those terms raises another, tantalising possibility: Would meaning itself be a good candidate for something which we feel—as in: is there a quale of meaning? A quale which, when present, indicates a degree of importance or relevance or certainty of our confidence in the verisimilitude[12] of the content to which it belongs[13].

Note that in all this talk of meaning I am using the word 'meaning' in a specific technical sense. My usage is not what one might find in the commonplace "That dog/cat/photo/engagement ring (or whatever) means something to me." Which is usually to convey that the dog/cat/photo/whatever has an emotional importance for me which I wish you as my interlocutor to know about. Rather, it is to say, when I see a sheep in a field, and the

---

12    We are taking truth to be a matter of a good or bad, better or worse, correspondence between the physical world and what we make of it. For mathematical and other abstract concepts, we must take confidence as some measure of how consistent our concept is, given our mathematical, or other, system of concepts, taken as a whole—some of which system might be verifiable by the external scrutiny, through discourse and demonstration of proofs etc. of others; but our conviction will be based on what we at any one time know, what we hold inside our heads.

13    Since as per MIMH a single quale might be delivered by a field of some astronomical number of gleeons, it is not inconceivable that such a field might constitute some percentage of gleeons mated with datums of (pure, as it were) Meaning.

surrounding hedge and a gate, I believe that what I see is
a sheep in a field, and real, because I have a special feeling
towards these things—a feeling that is intangible except
to say it is the realisation or the (understated but real
sense of) recognition I have—the feeling of confidence
I have, if you will—that the objects before me that I see
actually exist in the form, setting, and relative positions
in which I see them. For me to have such a feeling the
brain has generated qualia above and beyond mere shapes
focused on the back of the eye (i.e. which an artist might
report when drawing a sheep from life). Indeed, above
and beyond the mere associations that the brain might
attach to the word 'sheep': a diet of grass, the springy
texture of wool, etc. *Meaning(M)* carries with it the same
sense of conviction one has when one insists: "I know it is
a sheep," rather than: "I think it is a sheep."[14]

Running with this idea, if we ask: must a brain-like
system be conscious in order to deliver Meaning? We
would have to answer 'Yes' simply because Meaning,
taken as a whole, is an experience. Somehow, it is a kind of
feeling. It is a felt response to the clear and unambiguous
sighting of (say) the sheep in a field.

Extrapolating, if we ask: must a brain-like system be
conscious in order to have the concept of (for instance)
a sheep? Well, just how are *concept* and *meaning* related?

If Meaning is a feeling based on a sufficiency of neural
connectedness, then we can think of entertaining the
Concept[C] of a sheep if we achieve that sufficiency. It
would remain possible that a non-conscious brain could
achieve a sufficiency of connectedness which would give

---

14    A usual first approximation to what knowledge is is to say it is
'justified true belief' and while justified true belief in not in the end adequate
to the task of defining knowledge, its being facts to which we ascribe a special
and unusually strong certainty is made clear by 'justified true belief' and we
may now have a mechanism by which to explain the strength of feeling that
accompanies knowledge—especially if meaning is related to the number
and degree of affirmative associations available to Ideation and supportive of
some 'fact' or other.

it a similar degree of meaning (in a functional sense, lower case 'm'), and we might talk of the related concept (lower case 'c').

The presence of the white blob in the field means(m) a sheep is standing in the field when a sufficiency of indicators supports this explanation of the image projected onto the retina. The presence of the white blob Means(M) a sheep is standing in the field when that sufficiency occurs in a conscious brain and gives rise to qualia of Meaning(M).[15]

## A Conceptual Scale: putting the 'C' in Concept

We still have not said how we give content to a concept; we have merely suggested that Meaning(M) is a special attribute that might attach to a concept(c) when that concept is instantiated as part of a conscious mind.

We have hinted that a concept which is instantiated in Ideation is somehow given content by the neuron clusters which constitute it, and somehow and equally importantly given context by the association of those clusters to other clusters, both in Ideation and in Memory.

In MIMH we suggested that the ribbon of consciousness in the Lock Step model chased maximum meaning, focusing attention where neural connections and neural activity were densest, and following[16] associations to

---

15     Philosophers offer many and various theories of meaning. To some extent I do not mind what theory they subscribe to, allow me only that there are such things as qualia of meaning which arise when the content of any expression in their system of meaning is sufficiently well-formed and well-connected to mean something. Roughly, philosophers' theories of meaning seek to answer questions such as: How does the phrase "there is a sheep in the field" come to signify something to the mind/brain? How does the sight, sound and smell of a sheep in a field come to signify something to the human mind/brain? How can one mind/brain communicate to another mind/brain the fact of there being a sheep in a field?

16     For Ideation, 'following' can mean copy-pasting clusters from memory or from the sensory processing region into its dynamic neural space, i.e. based on associative links

produce an ever-changing pattern of activity.

Now we are similarly positing Meaning as arising when some threshold of connection count is reached (or in proportion to the size of the count—there is no reason to presuppose Meaning is a simple binary quality).

Indeed, we might wonder whether by providing enough context any need for content might go away; all that is needed is an array of suitably massively connected nodes. Real content is then defined by relative context. Each node at its most active might need do no more than give off a quale or some contributory fraction of a micro-quale, when stimulated.

Well, maybe (but there would have to be more to it. The whole story might involve an implementation like that shown in Figure 25, where memory is 'all spine').

But so far we have looked at the context of concepts in terms of Meaning(M) and studiously avoided content: where do concepts like wind and rain, sheep, field, gravity, airplane, earth, moon and sun, people, anger, grievance, rainbow, parachute, quantum theory, Hamlet, and King Arthur of Round Table fame, get their content from? Indeed what form of content can they all have that situates so easily (or in the case of 'quantum theory', less easily, perhaps) in the brain?

We have suggested that there has to be some raw topological equivalence between what we perceive (the unified, continuous world of our internal cinema) and the arrangement of qualia-producing clusters in Ideation (which may look like an elementary mistake, but is forced upon us in our need to avoid a homunculus who organises our experience in a meaningful way for us).

Why should we not go the whole hog as it were, in terms of topological real-world similarity, and compare the operation of Ideation to the 3D modelling used by a computer program in a 3D computer game?

We could conceive of a 3D computer game involving a

sheep in a field, enclosed by a hedge that is breached only by a red gate.

In such a game the sheep will be a single instantiation in computer memory of a class of object known as Sheep. The terms 'class' and 'object' are used in this example as technical computer programming terms. A *class* sets out the general properties of one general kind of a thing, like a sheep (or goat, or person). We can instantiate a *class* in our computer programme as an *object* and give each *object* a specific name so that we can refer to that instance, or object, uniquely inside the programme. The particular *object* which we insert into our hedge-bounded field and which takes its properties from the *class* Sheep might be given the name Larry.

Such named *objects* like Larry, all derived from the one *class*, Sheep, will have a set of procedures (or methods) in common. For instance, all *objects* derived from the *class* Sheep, will have the methods: walk, kneel, chew cud, bleat, blink, follow anything sheep-like, run from anything dog-like. While these are all behaviours, the Sheep *class* may also include methods related to its appearance on the computer screen (aka 'rendering'). For instance, there might be an instruction to display-from-left-hand-side or, more generally, display-from-viewpoint-angleX[17].

The field, hedge and gate may also be instantiations of their own *classes* of Field, Hedge and Gate.

There will have to be other procedures, or methods, in our 3D game for the game to work. For instance, there must be some kind of collision detection and reaction

---

17     Commonly 3D game engines will construct the 3D shapes of objects in their 3D world using hundreds or thousands of triangles, and render the triangles. But when objects are distant from the viewer in the game world, it pays not to render an element as ten thousand triangles merely to decide what colour to place in two or three pixels on-screen (with a computational overhead which is wholly lost and wasted), but to render the object as something simpler. It would then be sensible to ask the object 'How do you want to be rendered when viewed from the left at a virtual distance of 2 kilometres?

mechanism to prevent the sheep walking through the hedge. There must also be some kind of sense of gravity; were we initially to place the sheep 2 metres above the ground, it would need to fall towards the ground according to our calculation (part of the 3D game engine) of gravity's effect on it.

Of course our game model so far lacks any sense of language, so we could make sure it includes an augmented reality engine that taps into a database. When we hover the cursor over the sheep—or glance at it while wearing our eye-movement-detection goggles, the computer program issues a small pop-up with the summary of the sheep, its medical history, as per the game, threat level and so on...

Suppose we built such a model in Ideation, would that deliver an adequate conceptual model of our world?

First and foremost, as presented above, it is not flexible. It has been hard-wired as it were. We had to pre-create the game world: sheep on a hillside.

But that can be fixed.

We can envisage an apparatus which examines hillsides such as ours, identifies walls, fences and hedges, and identifies gates, as well as sheep, goats, donkeys, cattle etc. And this apparatus constructs a 3D model, just like that for a 3D computer game, which corresponds to the world of our hillside and also can be inserted, as that exact same 3D model, into Ideation.

This apparatus is obviously something of a homunculus itself, which we will have to watch out for but, more importantly, how is Ideation to make sense of the 3D world it now models?

Do we think that Ideation chooses a location in space in respect of the 3D model, and an angle of view towards the important contents inside the model (Figure 28), and it then *calculates* what the view should be (as it might appear on a 2D screen) and compares this view to the

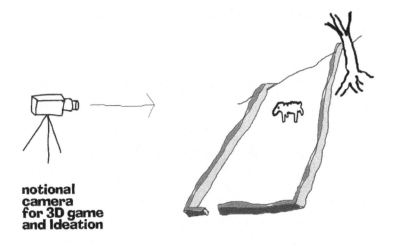

notional
camera
for 3D game
and Ideation

Figure 28. If we create a 3D model inside Ideation, a bit like the kind of 3D model you would expect inside a computer game, how does Ideation 'see' or (in computer terms) 'render' the model to get a 2D view?

image found in the sensory block?[18]

Well, suppose we had a non-homunculus world-building apparatus, and suppose we could load the 3D world model it created into Ideation, and suppose Ideation possessed effective 3D-world to 2D-view calculus, and suppose Ideation could effectively compare its 2D output to the data in the sensory block and they matched...

So what?

Wherein does meaning lie?

Some might say, meaning lies in the fact that we know that thus-and-such blob in the visual field is a sheep and sheep are like, this sort of mammal thing, like, and kinda white and fluffy, like, and eat the green stuff...

To which I retort (tartly, I might add): Fine, but how do you perceive all that? How do you give me the whole picture, as it were, in qualia, and with Meaning? (or even

18     The answer to my rhetorical question is undoubtedly, IMHO, no. But for the sake of pursuing this line of inquiry to its bitter end, let me assume, temporarily, the answer is, ahem, the opposite.

meaning(m), to be honest: in this picture I'd settle for meaning(m)).

Put another way: recreating an accurate representation of the whole 3D world inside Ideation demands a homunculus to make sense of it. And isn't the truth that in a computer game, we are the ones providing the meaning?

The other problem with the 3D game view of Ideation is how does the whole brain-ish mechanism learn anything new? (We must, of course deprive it of its homunculus teaching aid.)

How can it possibly learn what gravity is if we don't tell it in advance what the mathematical rules are? How can it master the notion of collision (or, more subtly, friction). How will it master ideas such as hot and cold, hunger and thirst, drought and drowning?

If it is entirely self-learning, the only tool available to it is the observed behaviour of objects and stuffs in the world. Possibly some behaviours will be of the stimulus-response kind. Others will seem unstimulated (An apple drops from a tree, unprovoked, and falls towards the ground).

Let us drop the idea of a 3D computer game model for Ideation[19]. Let us continue with our analysis of something perceptual, qualia-led, and flatter than anything it represents, because at least by taking that line we are pulling apart the mystery of meaning and concept and understanding in terms of elements that are constitutive of the brain and consciousness.

In this chapter we have poked and prodded concept and meaning, and we have touched on context and association, but we have ardently avoided content.

That, now, must change...

---

19      Since we need homunculi to create and to interpret the model.

# 8. Concept, Context and Content

We have spoken of meaning, and context, and associations, and suggested a mechanism by which Ideation could serve as a sandbox for dynamically manipulating concepts, but we have not pinned down exactly what a concept is.

We have suggested that concepts must be underpinned by one or many clusters of neurons, and that in many cases such a cluster will contribute to a quale of feeling.

But what is the content of a cluster of neurons such that it can deliver part or all of a concept?

We pressed meaning in two directions. In the first, meaning is a feeling which arises when a sufficiency of neural associations indicates a level of confidence in the validity of the content.

In the second, meaning is the object or idea to which some region of Ideation corresponds in the physical world or, at least, to some region of the brain other than itself[1].

What is our range of options for the nature of neural cluster content?

At the very minimum, our Ideation cluster might consist of a single neuron which, when it 'lights up', does no more than contribute one small micro-quale of feeling. It is a single pixel, as it were, in the cinema screen of our experience. Here, the meaning of the cluster must be conveyed entirely by its connections: its context and

---

1    This definition is intended to include in its scope purely conceptual systems, such as mathematics, or other ideas which take their truth and their meaning from a system of symbols. It also allows us to think meaningfully about our current experience and our current thoughts and allows us to derive meaning from sensory data which otherwise might merely imply the greater physical world.

its associations. But this does not explain very much, and suggests we are relying on the 'magic' of mysterious combinations of neural connections to explain how our conceptual machine works[2].

As a maximum (and thinking this way, there may be no maximum limit on size), a single Ideation cluster might represent the whole complete inclusive idea of a complex organism: a sheep, or a heart, a motor car, an ecosystem, or all of calculus.

Yet really what we need[3] is for each cluster to contain a single elemental concept object, a single component that does one useful job of work, contributing to any larger concept: it does one thing well—but it does something. And that something can be re-used to be incorporated into other ideas.

In the case of the human being as conceptual machine, I think we can in any case introduce some upper bounds on the possible range of concept size.

## Synaesthesia

For instance, the fact that some people suffer from (or enjoy) the condition of synaesthesia suggests that for most people Ideation clusters are dedicated to one kind of qualia generation: the majority of people see colours and hear sounds.

If, as happens in synaesthesia, people to some extent see sounds and hear colours, it suggests that where a sensory stimulus for the majority of people would prompt qualia of one kind, instead that stimulus prompts qualia of a different kind. This in turn suggests that sub-regions of neurons in Ideation are, for most people, dedicated to

---

2       You might even say we are relying on a homunculus who will step in and sort things out for us.
3       Our need is for something we have some hope of understanding; our hope is that a mechanism can be created which does the job and can be understood.

one or other type of sensory stimulus, but in synaesthesia, the sensory area for (say) audio processing is mis-wired, at least in part, to a region of Ideation that is dedicated to visualization.

For our purposes this points to a maximum possible granularity for clusters in Ideation—at least in terms of dedicated bands of operation: not all of Ideation can be used for any purpose[4].

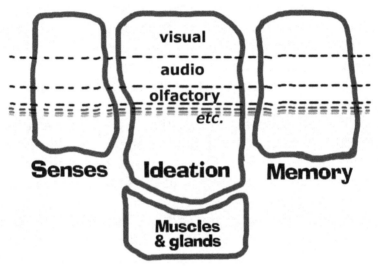

Figure 29. Banded Ideation: clusters in Ideation are dedicated to generating a specific kind of qualia, and these clusters are connected exclusively to memory and to sensory clusters related to those same kinds of qualia (It is a moot point for the time being whether Primary qualities may give rise to qualia. Also we have postulated that qualia of Meaning may be generated anywhere in Ideation).

---

4      A counter argument might go: any region of Ideation can generate any kind of qualia, and qualia-type is determined by data which accompanies whatever concept is being loaded into a cluster in Ideation. It is a data-type 'flag' in computing terms. And in synaesthesia it is the data flag which is lost or corrupted somewhere between sense input, memory and instantiation in Ideation. This may be true, but if we are seeking to reduce the complexity of the 'data' we process, we can do so nicely by designing it out via our architecture. If we cannot make our conceptual engine work, given this approach, we might have to reconsider.

## Generalization, the Abstract, and Creativity

Most of us, I think, are familiar with the idea of a square. We have the concept deeply embedded in our minds from our early school days[5].

And yet, when we see a square, it may be large or small, or seen from some oblique angle, or partially obscured. If I imagine a grey square with a red circle in it (I'm doing so now), how big is that? How much of my mind (of the internal film-screen that corresponds to my mind's eye) does it occupy? How does the thing imagined compare to the size of the computer screen before me? (In my case on this occasion, I would estimate, probably about a fifth of the size of the screen, with that 'measured' as a proportion of my field of view.)

The point I'm making is that when we encounter something in the world that is square, or has some noticeable component that is square, our brain/minds automatically fit our concept of the square to the square object, regardless of size.

Easily explained, many will say. The neural network that serves the eyes specifically filters signals coming from the eyes for easily-recognizable shapes. A square is fed to us, ready formed, from wherever it appears in the visual field, fresh and available for us to use.

Consider this (this is a true story and I'm sure a favourite trick of many lecturers):

In a lecture on noise in signals a lecturer displayed the Roman numeral II in black on a white projection screen. Slowly he introduced noise (in the form of a myriad of fine dots) and asked the class to raise their hands as soon as the letters were lost in the noise. Gradually, dutifully,

---

5          Perhaps 'idea' and 'concept' should mean slightly different things. An idea is perhaps best thought of as the instantiation in my brain/mind of a concept that can be articulated beyond my brain/mind—although I'm not sure this distinction serves any useful purpose in the current text.

the class came, in the end, all to have their hands raised.

Then he reversed the process, asking that we lower our hands as soon as we could see the II return from the noise.

The class, eagerly, lowered their hands, only in the end to discover that it was not a II that had returned but a III that was now on view. The point the lecturer was trying to make being: *We create what we want to see from an insufficiency of data.*

In terms of the square of my example, my point is, I impose a square shape on whatever insufficiency I get from my senses: Where do I keep my idealized representation of a square and how do I adjust that ideal form to make it fit the inadequate data from my senses?

Which is to say, I have somehow encoded the concept of square, and it is encoded in such a way that I can generate a square of any size or orientation (rotation or oblique angle of view) from it[6].

This question might be framed in terms of artificial neural networks where some core (say) image data in a deeply hidden layer can be used to generate variations on the theme of the original image. The encoded data is likely not recognisable to the human eye as representing the image, but such an encoded image might offer the abstract representation of the concept that the original image represented, and allow that abstraction to be stored in memory, and be turned into a useful instance of the concept (a useful variation of the original) whenever fetched from memory, or contributing to an idea (of either an insufficiently well defined image originating in the eyes, or part of a pure idea as contemplated ex nihilo within Ideation).

---

6       The alternative would be to say the concept of square is full and complete and rigid and fixed and it is the comparison process which dynamically deals with imperfect comparisons.

One plausible candidate for the content of a cluster of Ideation neurons might then be the encoded form of a shape or sound or other sensorily-derived entity, as is found in artificial neural networks.

Two difficulties come to mind with this approach.

**General Decoding**

In artificial neural networks we are used to the decoding process having had similar training as the encoding process, which is to say the decoding is not like (say) a general purpose zero-loss unzip function, rather decoding is a process that must itself have been trained on similar data to the original encoder.

So if we lean on the methods of artificial neural networks, either we are going to have to carry our decoder network alongside the encoded data, or we have to invent a single decode-anything network that sits on top of Ideation, that may serve as a final 'output stage' prior to qualia generation. But this would not work because of pattern matching and searching[7]. If you remove structure from data by encoding it, you have to decode it whenever you search for structures or patterns that have been obscured by the encoding.

**Search and compare**

A criterion we must impose on our cluster content, whether in memory, sensory processing, or in Ideation, is that we can search for it in memory by its essential features and compare it to the data in some neural cluster arriving from the senses, or formed in Ideation.

In some sense either features must be readable

---

7        As a result of which we would need to insert a homunculus to inspect, interpret and act on everything seen in this output, which is of course our internal cinema screen

after any encoding we perform, or features must be incorporated into the search mechanism we use to store and locate items in memory.

We might envisage encoding occurring when sensory signals arrive from the senses[8] and, thereafter, until qualia are generated, all the internal processing of the brain/mind is performed on the encoded form of the data.

But when we think here of abstracted encoded data (as we might produce internally inside an artificial neural network), how are we to store and locate such encoded data in memory, or indeed perform any useful comparison or other functional tasks upon the fully realised ideas in that data unless the data is decoded to a recognisable (to us) form, every time it is referenced?

When I think of a house from outside, I can zoom in consciously to any feature, from chimney top to window sill. Are we going to claim that every such operation in the brain involves a decoding operation as (I believe) happens on a computer drive that has been compressed: every write-to and every read-from the drive passes through a compression/decompression process?

Which is to say, we cannot simply decode the data at output (i.e. to qualia, for clear perceptions); decoded data is needed within Ideation. Indeed decoded data is needed within the sensory block since we have to compare what we generate in Ideation with what we seem to be receiving from the senses (the lecturer's II versus III example).

Does this mean that we must use raw data everywhere?

Perhaps not. What we do need is a form of encoding which allows us both to decode in a flexible way to an idea that can be shaped or guided in its final form by context, but also an encoding which overtly preserves key features of the original idea.

---

8      It must happen to some extent in any case, even if just a pattern of activation to indicate such-and-such rod or cone in the retina has fired, or such-and-such hair in the inner ear has started vibrating.

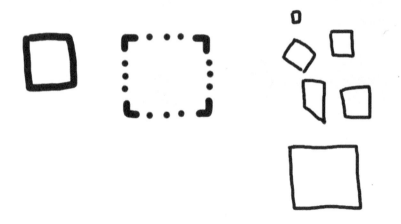

Figure 30. The elasticated memory of a square. Left - the original source square; Middle - the square in memory; Right - shapes matched by Ideation to squares given the 'recipe for a square' that is stored in memory.

A rather trivial and unlikely example might be the treatment of a square in Figure 30.

Let us call this *Flexible Feature Encoding*, where we incorporate some must-haves or key features (the corners) unencoded into our data entity, and any more elastic requirements or flexible features (same length sides, and parallel sides) as overt place-holders or sense-specific variables[9].

There may be mathematical approaches to Flexible Feature Encoding [FFE], but let us suppose as our starting point that the Key Features in FFE are just those patterns which are normally identified in the sensory processing region which are hard-wired into sensory processing either from by Nature or by Nurture, but they are relatively (if not entirely) permanent and necessary features for our sensory processing to work.

---

9        A sense-specific variable might be a line of variable length, or any colour, for vision; it might be any continuous tone for sound; of course omitting a feature amounts to a wildcard whereby that feature is not needed for the essence of the item, for instance a memorial plaque on a park bench.

Possibly FFE is wrong and all that is needed is Key Feature Encoding.

It is easy to envisage how a rectangle might be recognised (via approximations as needed) from four corners. Easy also for an oval. But do we ever recognise a square or a circle in quite the same way?

Being a square or a circle imposes very strict mathematical rules on a rectangle or oval. One might argue that, taking the shape down to an atomic level (painting in atoms) these shapes are never truly realised (not least because everything is always in motion, but in principle because any two atoms are neither joined by 'dots' or an inked line, nor are they themselves shaped (as a pair) as either the curve of some specific macro scale circle, or the corner or edge of a square—or rectangle either)...

The point being: we can only decide a rectangle is a square by examining it closely, thinking about it and possibly taking measurements[10]. Where am I going with this? As follows: the basic pattern, I suggest, is the rectangle or oval, which can be loosely represented, and the upgrade to a circle or square is achieved by a cognitive process, that is to say either by reason or by the application of some number of additional pattern matching criteria.

Doing it this way means we do not have to encode the flexible components; flexibility comes from additional processing, what we might call the Processing To Refinement of a more general pattern.

## What the eyes see and what the I sees

There is a troubling (for me) philosophical question that hangs over this current discussion. An assumption I have made is that what counts as a feature of any kind is clear and unambiguous.

---

10      To some extent the same can be said of a rectangle or oval, but less so; we need less precision to justify calling something rectangular or oval.

I have suggested (which I expect many to baulk at, but is a consequence of the Lock Step model) that the topology of qualia in Ideation corresponds to the topology of the cells in our brains that produce them. Which is to say the shapes we see in the cinema screen of our inner mental life corresponds to the arrangement of qualia-producing cells in the brain, and the implication is (in all I have been arguing about above) that this is the same as the topology of images that arrive on the retina.

However we already accept that the secondary qualities which we perceive do not exist in the objects in the world that we perceive (My Bic Biro is not blue. It has no colour. It merely emits photons of light at certain wavelengths, when illuminated, which when they arrive on the back of my eye trigger events in my brain which lead me to experience the colour blue in my mental field of vision).

When we look at an image produced by a lens on a sheet of paper and see the image is an inverted and reflected representation of the field of view of the lens, we might ask 'what is really projected on the paper?'

You may think it is obvious, since we can experimentally verify and explain by ray-drawing, that what appears in the piece of paper is the inverted/reflected image of the scene available to the lens.

But, both the scene before the lens, and the image on the paper are all and only what *we* perceive. All three images (scene, paper, perception) are the product of our perceptual processes. If we are analysing these images with a view to designing a conceptual apparatus that manipulates them (or sounds or anything else senses-wise) what reason do we have for thinking anything we see, perceive or process has any real basis in reality?

Why is this a worry? A general purpose conceptual machine will not be a general purpose machine; we risk designing ourselves into it.

**Searching, size, and complexity**

We can recognize dogs, cats, elephants, giraffes, as well as designer brands such as Mercedes, Ferrari, Porsche and Jaguar.

These are objects whose listed Key Features need not always be present, and we introduce the idea of what philosophers might call family resemblance (the family taken as a whole displays a range of distinct features although each family member may only display a subset of these features, nonetheless the subset is large enough to easily group each individual with the rest of the family).

The net effect is not entirely dissimilar to what psychologists call *gestalt*; we recognise a cat because, taken as a whole, the creature before us is more cat than dog, and definitely not giraffe or rhinoceros.

However this level of complexity, the gestalt of a cat, strikes me as the most complex idea we can hold, or need to hold, in a neural cluster.

If we want to think about details, about ears, eyes, paws etc. then we need another cluster that captures the essence of those. The more general representation of the cat will reference the detailed representation of the ear via associative links.

This in turn suggests that associations can exist from sub-regions of a concept (pixel-level) not, as has been assumed up until now, from the whole concept per se.

This in turn would require us to revise our memory model. We would need to be able to form associations from component parts of our memory cluster—but does that not undermine, if not break, our model for memory: one of distinct usable components?

Figure 31 shows the sort of associative linkage we would need.

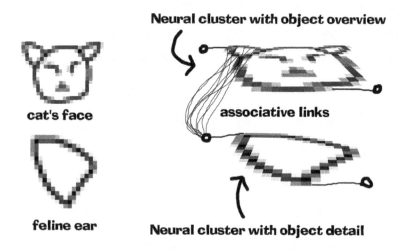

**Neural cluster with object overview**

**cat's face**

**associative links**

**feline ear**

**Neural cluster with object detail**

Figure 31. Neural clusters in memory (and also as may be copied into Ideation) are multiply associatively linked to facilitate drilling down or zooming in on a specific feature or aspect.

Let us take a step back.

What we are after is, at base, simplicity. We need to be able to construct complexity from simple components because, after all, that is what we are going to end up doing in Ideation, in concept generation, and surely concepts are constructed bottom up, not top down[11].

Consider one of those puzzles where you are asked: what is the difference between the two drawings? And you are told (say) that there are four differences, as per Figure 32.

How do I go about spotting the difference?

---

11      We may learn about ears top down, through perceptions; we see many animals, all are complex objects to our senses, and we come to notice ears, after which we can identify ears, so we learn about features of a complex world by repeated exposure to the things those complexes of features (animals) have in common. But those special features are then etched into our brain/minds and work with the common features of any new animal we subsequently perceive *to construct the world*. Again the question of why not place qualia generation at the back of the eye? Because it would Mean nothing; we have to re-construct the world for ourselves for it to Mean anything; we can only construct it from [small] component parts.

Figure 32. *Can you spot the difference?* puzzle.

Here of course there is great scope for individual differences; for people to go about the task in vastly different ways. So here I shall stubbornly restrict my discussion to letting you know how I go about it[12].

When I do these puzzles I glance at the whole, first one panel, then the other, and see if I can spot in my general impression of each what might be different. For me, this approach would probably yield the fact that the chimney positions are different. Then, knowing that there are three more feature differences, I would home in or different regions of the picture in turn, and compare the two pictures for those specific features: each of the windows, the door and the gate. This would deliver the different patterns of glazing in the front door and the

---

12      Richard Feynman in the YouTube Video linked below starting 2:30 minutes in, discusses how we can have vastly different individual ways of tackling a problem [https://youtu.be/Si6NbKqYEd8 "Way of Thinking by Richard Feynman" on Channel "The Cosmological Reality" confirmed April 17 2023]. There may be such great variation in individual approaches to problem solving that experimentally identifying the most common approach, or some average approach, provides no usable insight. All we need for now, above, is a single approach that, taken as a whole, works.

different number of lines representing the horizontals of the gate.

Finally, searching for my fourth difference, I would look at the vehicle. This, as it happens, I scan from right to left (i.e. windscreen first) and notice that, comparing one against the other as my focus of interest travels leftward, I come to the rear of the vehicle and discover that the rear window is missing in the right hand panel.

What use can I make of my anecdotal observation? Well, at any one time I am looking for simple differences, and I deliberately restrict the focus of my attention to aspects of the picture with only a few features, and compare those features—typically five or fewer, for some detailed difference.

It is as if that is the best I can do; I, personally, can only compare up to five features at a time. A simple (some might say simplistic) explanation would be to say that the images in my Ideation block[13] when I conduct my survey typically contain five or fewer features. Thus I conclude that the granularity of neural clusters in my Ideation supports [visual] patterns of the same order of magnitude (i.e. less than ten Key Features).

If this is true then my high level (most abstract) pattern for a face might be an oval with two eyes, possibly with the luxury of a mouth, nose and two ears... Might that not be the case, not only for me but more generally?

The suggestion that the highest order of abstractions we make of human faces, of dogs, cats and so on are no more complex than child-like line drawings may initially sound as naive as the suggestion that qualia must be topologically arranged physically as we perceive them. But it may not be so wide of the mark when one considers not merely children's early years' artistic renditions of the world around them, but also the rendering of ideas which

---

13     Were I to model my human brain in the brain-ish architecture I am developing in this text.

Figure 33. Naive representations.

human beings have used in the past, in for example Egyptian hieroglyphs, Mayan and other art.

This is not to say that the art of the time was not elaborate, but it seems to me that effort was made to identify and incorporate the key identifying features of various creatures, which allowed them to be instantly recognisable.

This is speculative, of course, but all I need in order to make my case in favour of the conceptual machine I am constructing, is that such suggestions are plausible; such an idea does not contain contradictions and does not fatally flaw the project, and indeed, actually seems to further the detailed development of the project[14].

Suppose then, we accept that the content of any cluster in Ideation is rarely more complex than (for a visual

---

14    That is to say: this is a philosophical/computational experiment not a psychological or biological inquiry. The goal of the experiment is to see how a conceptual machine (i) might plausibly work, (ii) how it might be instantiated electronically or in software, and (iii) how it might be controlled. The tests of success or failure in the end will be ones of 'Does the conceptual machine work?' and 'Can I regulate its behaviour with regard to truth-telling and a moral code?'

component) (say) a 24 pixel by 24 pixel visual field[15].

We are getting some sense of size, here, although we are left with questions about how to associate details within an image to their expanded, zoomed-in, more comprehensive counterparts.

If I have the impression of a cat in my field of view and I look again more closely and check (say) its left ear (on the right of the head from where I am looking), how does Ideation link to the more detailed ear cluster that should be available to it from memory? (Figure 31)

Which is to say: how is the cluster in Ideation organised so that qualia topology is veridical and at the same time zooming-in[16] on a specific feature works seamlessly?

Let us go full-on-naive. Suppose the neurons in a cluster form a two-dimensional array, pixel-like, which could receive and respond to a serial FT-list, and any

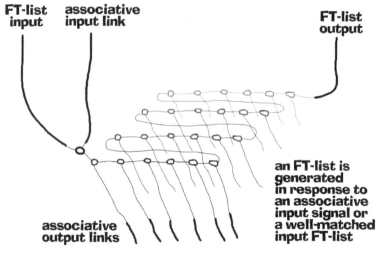

**FT-list input**    **associative input link**          **FT-list output**

an FT-list is generated in response to an associative input signal or a well-matched input FT-list

**associative output links**

Figure 34. Naive memory cluster.

---

15      Not that we think in pixels, but I wish to indicate a level of distinguishable detail. How we might determine what is needed for audio and other senses remains to be seen.

16      To *zoom-in* we request and load the content of associative links from memory.

neuron in the array can both contribute to a quale and have an association to any other element of memory.

Several pixel-neurons in the naive image of a cat face will link to 'ears'. If a cat-face is activated via a search request, 'ears' will automatically be multiply associated with a number of pixel-neurons in the image, and finer detail of an ear can easily be loaded if Ideation follows such associative links as part of a zoom-in process[17].

We are now invited to diverge from our earlier model of a memory cluster as being a connective topology of neurons—a topology for topology's sake—to being one of an array[18] of neurons where the FT-list no longer has to represent connectivity[19], but can be used simply to address and extract serialised data from a cluster.

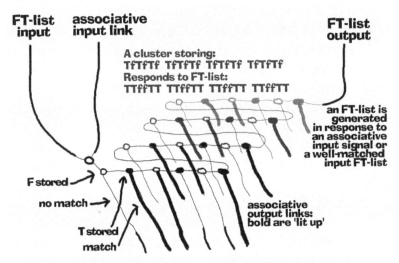

Figure 35. Naive memory cluster with nodes 'lit up' where they match a newly loaded FT-list, and consequently activate their associative links.

---

17    As suggested earlier, multiply associated (referenced) memory clusters are loaded preferentially over singly or sparingly referenced clusters.
18    Of dimensions and a dimensionality commensurate with the type sense data being stored. 2D for visual. 1D for audio. Possibly 0D for olfactory
19    We can still envisage there being a compressed, spatially efficient encoding that uses connectiveness to reduce the number of neurons needed, but that would be an optimization of our basic, functional-if-rather-slow model.

Figure 35 shows how a naive memory cluster might operate when an FT-list on the input port matches the content of the cluster:

A 'good match' between the static content of the cluster (dark circles are storing Ts and light circles are storing Fs) and the incoming FT-list causes the associative link (the trailing lines) for each of the matched cells (the circles) to be activated.

Possibly, of course, the associative links should only ever 'fire' when the FT-list exactly matches the cluster content. When that happens, they all fire.

Possibly, some associative links will fire whenever their parent cell is matched.

The naive cluster system is capable of reacting to close matches, if we want to tune it to do that.

Whatever implementation details we may later decide are necessary, we have at least moved our overall brain-ish architecture forward. And although we have adopted what might be called naive design options, we might prefer to think of them as 'simple' and in accordance with Occam's Razor.

They do at least promise the possibility of making the internal operations of the brain-ish machine visible from outside.

We do however need to think about how these memory clusters are re-assembled in Ideation i.e. to make sense.

However that may not be a difficult problem since an important contextual element is supplied by the incoming sense data which is triggering these memory components (in parallel), so the bigger picture develops in parallel.

Otherwise, when purely conceptual thinking is being undertaken the combination of clusters that are extracted from memory will be guided by associations between clusters (while being over-ridable by cognitive decision-making, or 'will' if you will, or what strikes the current focus of attention as being of most interest (see MIMH on

Free Will and Determinism)). Absent of will, memories bring their own (cluster) context.

At the start of this chapter we asked the question: *What is the content of a cluster of neurons such that it can deliver part or all of a concept?*

We now have an answer, that for our purposes content can be a naive fragmentary representation, both in Ideation[20] and in Memory, and built up from component fragments that are readable directly from the Sensory block, where pattern memory has been inherited or learned (or a bit of both).

We have been thinking about 2-dimensional visual data. Can we generalise it to audio, to taste and smell and other senses?

I think the answer is going to be *yes* for all the secondary qualities, except that I think we still need to say something about primary qualities: extension, motion etc. and not least motion, since we need to find a way to accommodate behaviour into our conceptual model since some representation of behaviour is needed for any dynamic system[21].

Behaviour is about change and, taking a naive approach as elsewhere in this text, I might ask: Can all behaviour be captured, simply, as a series of possible or likely changes in the static representation of the form[22] already present in the Perception, Memory, Ideation model?

Will behaviour turn out, as would be consistent with our naive brain-building, to be a variation of Wile E. Coyote[23] running beyond the cliff edge?

---

20    We will have to revisit our Switch Register architecture for Ideation.
21    In the sense that the content the system represents is dynamic, not that the system itself when operating is dynamic, which of course it is.
22    Shape, pattern, 'object', idea.
23    A cartoon character created by Chuck Jones and Michael Maltese in 1948 for Warner Bros.

# 9. Time Is the Ghost of the Next Thing That Might Happen

We have come to some idea of the granularity of Memory and of Ideation, based on the fundamental elements that (at least for vision) are picked out from an incoming visual signal, and are assembled in a simple way.

We have also proposed that content is encoded using a naive cell-wise representation, which approximates to the idea of pixels in an image. But in order to support this we need individual pixel 'cells' inside memory to be associated with any cluster anywhere in memory, as implied in Figures 34 and 35.

This requires that we reconsider not only how Memory is structured, but also how Ideation is structured, because a large burden on this system now falls on how a memory cluster (with so many associative links) and how Ideation (with the same number and pattern of associative links) can be formed, and copied.

For instance, if we have the face of a cat in a 24 by 24 cell array, and we want to follow the association with the ear, we need each pixel of the cat's ear to be associated with the memory cluster for such ears, Figure 31.

However, at the same time, none of the other requirements we have placed on memory has changed. We still need to be able to search for memory clusters using FT-lists, and copy clusters using FT-lists. We need to be able to activate a memory when addressed, and for it to activate its associative links when it is addressed, and for it to issue its full FT-list when addressed. What mechanism will support this new burden of cell-by-cell

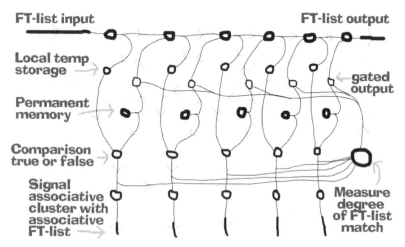

Figure 36. Updated memory cluster (only 5 cells big for illustration). Arrows show the direction of data flow. An 'F' or a 'T' will be passed in the direction that each arrow indicates.

associativity?

We are going to impose one further constraint, which is not unreasonable for biological or electronic or software based systems, which is that the cells we use are like perceptrons: they have multiple inputs and a single output.

The result is shown in Figure 36.

Talking through the new memory cluster: An FT-list is placed on the Memory block input port and broadcast to all of memory.

In the cluster of Figure 36, the serial FT-list arrives and is shifted, left-to-right, along the top row of cells and by the time the full list is loaded the local temporary storage cells (second row) contain a copy of the list.

At this point a cell by cell comparison is made (fifth row), between the temporary storage cells (second row) and permanent storage cells (fourth row) and:

(i) any matching cell issues (broadcasts) the FT-list for the memory cluster associated with that particular cell (via bottom row), and (ii) the sum of all matching cells is taken (fifth row, far right), to give a measure of the agreement between the incoming FT-list and the stored FT-list.

If a 'good match' threshold is reached then the gated output cells (third row) are instructed to release the memory cluster's full, clean, FT-list into the neural stream which feeds Memory's output port.

(FT-lists for the associative links (bottom row) can be stored in Switch Registers, not shown.)

This replicates the functionality we had for memory before, except that this time any match for even part of the memory cluster will generate associative responses for those parts that match.

However, with this model, we need a systematic way of adding and changing associative links, since the associative links, now that they are part of the internal structure of the cluster, can no longer be managed by simply changing the inter-cluster wiring inside the Memory block[1].

To this end we need to think of how memories are initially formed.

Initially, high order patterns (e.g. a cat's face) will be processed through the Sensory block on many occasions, and will time and again be decomposed by that block into component shapes for ears, eyes, mouth etc. Ideation, reading the Sensory block, will send the FT-list for the cat face into Memory and see what comes back.

The first few times of encountering a cat, nothing will come back, so what actually needs to be sent into Memory[2] *every time* is the FT-list for the new cat face plus

---

1    Contextual associative links will continue to operate on the macro scale, from cluster to cluster, connecting clusters, and treating clusters as separate entities.

2    Because when data is collected from the Sensory block, neither the Sensory block nor Ideation know whether the Memory block knows about cats, and thus every occasion of a memory-call will be treated as a if the data is a new phenomena, a completely new thing (or the same thing with important new features), and so each call must contain all that is needed to

the FT-lists for its recognised component parts (ears, eyes, mouth etc.). If Memory repeatedly gets requests for the new FT-list which it cannot satisfy, at some point it will create a new cluster taking its content from[3] the new FT-list and with separate FT-lists for each of the component parts either recognised by Ideation or elemental shapes from the Sensory block.

There is now the problem of how to make sure that the FT-list for each component part ends up associated with the correct 'pixel' cell in the original image i.e. that thus-and-such FT-list belongs to one component part and not another. (The cat's ear in the cat's face of Figure 31 is associated only with memory clusters for feline ears, and so on, for eyes, mouth etc.)

The trick here is to include a pixel placement mask prior to each FT-list. In a 3x3 array, a pixel placement mask indicating that the 3rd and 6th pixels need to be associated with an FT-list of, say, ffffTTTTffffTTTT, would be ffTffTfff.

Thus the full search instruction from the Sensory block and Ideation into Memory would have the form:

**<FT-list for main image>**<mask for image component #1>**<FT-list for associative link for all elements in mask #1>**<mask for image component #2>**<FT-list for associative link for all elements in mask #2>**

...and so on until all the recognised components in the original image have been included.

When it comes to Ideation, each cluster in Ideation will have a similar internal structure to clusters in Memory, i.e. to reproduce our 'naive cell array', although the question of how Ideation clusters are combined and how they change now needs addressing.

---

lay down a fresh memory. A refinement being that the fine detail will be at the end of the FT-list sequence, and can and will be ignored if there is already a good match for the key features from the list(s) in Memory.

3          And thereby automatically indexed by, or keyed on.

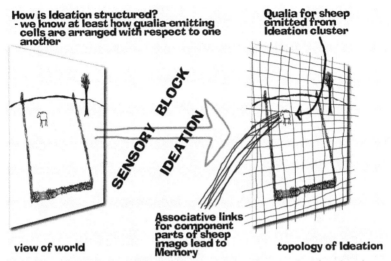

Figure 37. The topology of qualia-emitting clusters in Ideation is given to us by our own personal experience.

Ideation clusters for the sheep are 'above' the Ideation clusters for the gate and are 'to the left of' ideation clusters for the tree. This does not mean that qualia emitting clusters are arranged in a plane, nor that the set of qualia emitting clusters is fixed; qualia emitting clusters might occupy a complex 3D surface inside any brain, and the active surface may shift from moment to moment.

We have already imposed one constraint on how Ideation is structured since we have insisted that the topology of qualia-emitting clusters must correspond to the continuous, unbroken apparently smooth topology of the cinema screen world as we perceive it through our inner eye, Figure 37 (and Figure 27 in Chapter 7).

While qualia emission may guide us toward the overall relative arrangement of clusters, we have to ask how are they connected to each other and what other clusters may exist or be needed between them?

When we populate the visual qualia-emitting clusters in Ideation, we are recreating the image that is projected on the retina at the back of the eye (albeit reflected and inverted, and we have two eyes, and our eyes are forever moving in saccades, etc.), except that in Ideation any recognisable components parts in the scene before us are given Meaning by being linked to possibly thousands of sensations, concepts, behaviours and emotions that are associated with that object (or to other constituents of the scene).

This process arises because the Sensory block must not only recognise and pick out shapes from the visual field, but also locate those shapes in the visual field so that the visual field as a whole can be re-assembled in Ideation, with Meaning[4].

At first blush our location mechanism could be an FT-list *mask*, as is used for identifying the component parts of a memory cluster for which associative links are to be attached—although this mechanism might be hugely inefficient in terms of bandwidth. Let us roll with it for now, see if in principle something like this could work, and then revisit it later to optimise it[5].

So, what else do we need to be able to do in Ideation?

We need to be able to connect objects and regions from our visual field to data associated with them at a macro level. For instance a sheep will likely be associated with the general pattern of the heard word 'sheep', the visual representation of the word 'sheep', as well as with the muscle instructions to the tongue, mouth and lungs to speak the word 'sheep'.

Also, we need to capture and play out behaviours, and sometimes we need those behaviours to involve interactions with other, perhaps distant, elements in the world view—or maybe even outside the world view, hidden, or out of sight, but known about and still able to influence the behaviour of visible elements in our scene.

Equally, each object will need to be able to *react*,

---

4          Meaning (M) for a qualia-generating biological system, meaning(m) for a non-qualia generating system.
5          Alternatively, for instance, could we rely on the order in which information is extracted to indicate location? E.g. by having the order of data collection spiraling out from the centre of the visual field?

behaviourally (in character as it were) to events initiated by other objects in the field of view (or out of it).

If we know a boy is hiding behind the tree; if we know a crow has just wandered out of sight on the far side of the sheep; if we know a fox is running along the far side of the hedge, having just passed the other side of the gate; if there is a bird in the tree and we can hear it sing but not see it; or if the sheep jumps without notice, we infer the presence of an unseen predator, and so on...

Some elements in the scene will be known to us, or suspected by us, but not visible. Do we imbue them with no visible qualia, but allow them (say) primary qualities such as shape, extension, and motion?

Where and how do we connect these non-visible or unseen elements to the qualia-bearing elements in Ideation?

Especially when the qualia-bearing elements maintain an apparently homogeneous surface—only in physical trauma is the world we perceive ever distorted i.e. to become a horror show[6] (like the face in Edvard Munch's *The Scream*). There is only so much physical-mechanical disruption or discontinuity that the qualia-bearing elements can tolerate before failing to work as they should.

So, with regard to the non-visible elements, we need to be able to insert any number of them into Ideation to be in effect 'masked' behind their visible counterparts[7]. Should they become visible such elements might easily be accommodated into the physical qualia surface in their correct position[8].

---

6        I am grateful to Katarina Hudson, 1961-2022, for this horrendous insight.

7        Since Ideation space is not merely three-dimensional but is capable of multi-dimensional connectivity, we might simply insert them along another dimension, although that might remove any 'experience' of them—i.e. any other-than-visible qualia—from the vicinity where they are needed.

8        Subject to errors of visual illusion etc. so 'correct' here really means best guess, but that is true of probably every element in Ideation.

(However, this insertion of elements or clusters in another plane is reminiscent of building up a 3D world by allocating objects to different grid reference points. This is deeply unsatisfactory because if we start thinking like that we invite the need for a homunculus to interpret the scene.)

Let us remind ourselves that qualia are all we need, so long as the qualia include the assertion of individual objects in the world by their[9] bearing Meaning.

If the objects and the qualia do not bear Meaning then we need a homunculus to interpret them and we are back to square one with our whole perceptual/conceptual model/machine. It feels as though the model we are building in Ideation is getting more and more like a 3D computer game world and we are extracting a qualia viewing plane from it—with labels from an augmented reality engine.

This feels like a mistake in the making, but does the feeling come from anything other than the fact that we are constructing an architecture and processes that will generate a world view, and that is what a 3D games does, albeit in an entirely different way[10]?

Nonetheless, the nagging feeling is, that by doing no more than generating qualia, we are simply re-presenting data from the senses to a homunculus which needs, then, to interpret it. So let us remind ourselves: we have *given* the data an interpretation (via associations and context) and we have *added* a feeling of satisfaction that our interpretation at any one time is sufficient. This constitutes Meaning, and thus we should ask: What more *could* a homunculus do, or add, to satisfy the question of how a consciousness comes into being and makes sense of the world?

---

9        The objects and the qualia

10       A 3D computer game might typically use a 'viewing frustrum' to define the view required of the game world and use a 'projection matrix' to calculate how those things in the view are to be 'rendered' on the screen.

The point is, at the end of all our processing, the only thing we want left for our minimal homunculus[11] to do is feel[12].

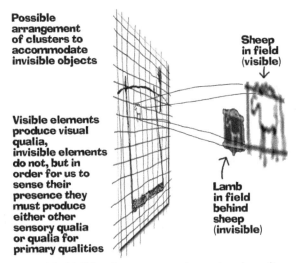

**Possible arrangement of clusters to accommodate invisible objects**

**Sheep in field (visible)**

**Visible elements produce visual qualia, invisible elements do not, but in order for us to sense their presence they must produce either other sensory qualia or qualia for primary qualities**

**Lamb in field behind sheep (invisible)**

Figure 38. Visible elements produce visual qualia, non-visible elements do not, but in order for us to sense the presence of non-visible elements they must produce either other sensory qualia or qualia for primary qualities.

We briefly see the tail of a lamb, guess it is a lamb, and insert the idea of a lamb into the visual field, but somehow it is not illuminated; we sense only its dimensionality 'round the corner' as it were. Where and how do we plumb in the Ideation data cluster for the lamb?

How do we plumb in the lamb (Figure 38)?

Suppose it is half-behind the sheep. We can see the lamb's tail and we infer and mentally construct the rest of the creature behind the sheep. We must morph and grow the sheep shape to become 'sheep part-concealing lamb'. Possibly at great distances we have only the personal verbal commentary of a third party: "I think there's a lamb behind the sheep." But if we are closer, so that details of

---

11    The mated gleeon-datum pair that gives rise to a micro-quale.

12    It must not have to think or process anything; it is a homogeneous surface of qualia.

the sheep are visible and elements of lamb and elements of sheep are physically interspersed, those features must be interspersed among Ideation clusters. At the same time they must be 'wired together' by associative links to maintain the wholeness (unity) of each: a whole sheep and a whole lamb. This feels like a cluster-management nightmare.

Maybe all we can do is sub-vocally comment, "There is a lamb behind the sheep," or "There is a fox running along the far side of the hedge," and *if* we visualise either, then we visualise them in clusters that are physically adjacent those used for the visible hedge, but imagined[13] and not fully 'rendered' in qualia.

That way, we never actually build a full 3D model which places them out of the live qualia plane. In which case a part-showing lamb is just that, part of a lamb-cluster that happens to be visible, and which we can (using our imagination as just mentioned) visualise as a lamb by an effort of overlaying the rest of the speculated creature over the requisite part of the sheep.

In this way we can do away with 3D world-building, and treat the plane of the qualia as, if not flat, then at least a surface. When we imagine something, that something can co-exist alongside things evidenced from the Sensory block, but our imagined somethings are sparse and require effort to focus on (to load temporarily into qualia-producing clusters) and will (sadly for the design engineer) require more complex cluster management.

So now that we can accommodate our partially- or non-visible objects in the field of view how do we give

---

13     We are inventing the process of 'imagined' as a weaker qualia generator, or a qualia generator that is distributed sparsely across the active qualia-producing surface. We (our brains) can focus on the lamb (fox or whatever) and load clusters, bring the lamb to more prominence, and visualize it, as if in front of the sheep. But the pressure of live data from the Sense block will constantly try to drive back our imagined lamb, out of sight. It is an effort to think about it, hiding behind the sheep.

them, or indeed the fully visible objects, behaviours?

What are behaviours?

For sheep, behaviours might be walking, grazing, turning in a circle. For objects in the world in general, behaviours might include falling under gravity, puffing up cheeks, changing colour, scratching head, a car door opening, water spraying from a sprinkler, ink mixing into water, a rubber ball distorting on impact, a hammer stopped by a nail[14].

We can view behaviours that play out within a cluster as simple changes in the data (pixels) of the cluster. If a sheep turns, bodily, to face us, the behaviour plays out through a series of changes to its profile (I'm thinking fairly distant sheep here. One that may demand relatively few clusters to represent it).

Thus it would seem that any cluster representing object behaviour should be associated directly with the cluster for the object.

It might be tempting to make them co-extensive i.e. have them weave in and out of each other to achieve closest proximity. However there is no reason to suppose all possible behaviours of some object can be accommodated in the same Ideation space as the object itself. That is to say, for any single object, behaviours may be (next to) unlimited[15].

There remains the question of whether behaviours (if thought of as a series of animated frames) are realised by fetching new, changed 'frames' from Memory, or in some algorithmic way (e.g. sheep body grows thinner when

---

14    One might draw a distinction here between the gross, mass or wholesale movement of an object achieved by moving the object's representation to an adjacent cluster in Ideation, and having the object's representation within a cluster change. A man might walk; a face might redden.

15    And our brain-ish massively multi-linked neuralesque machine can incorporate an indefinite number of behaviours as an indefinite number of dimensions linked to our cluster in Ideation—well, OK, we suggested a limit of 1000 links earlier, but we could cascade links...

viewed end-on).

Since the brain does not run the algorithms that would be run on 3D objects in a computer game, and since learning from experience is going to be extensive for our conceptual engine, it seems to me that the safer bet (and all that is needed) is for behaviour clusters to replay sequences of 'views' of the real object, or a closely similar object, from memory.

If this is so, a single behaviour cluster could be no more than a normal cluster where the 'pixel' cells are associated with one of a series of behavioural frames.

How would a behaviour be triggered, and why one behaviour rather than another?

(Let us recall what we are trying to do here: We have extracted visual sensory data and reconstructed the scene before the eye, but now with Meaning. The scene before the eye changes, and we try to match the change to what we think is going on, i.e. that a behaviour is playing out.

Once the sheep is established in Ideation, and is, say, walking, as it takes a step, the Sensory block delivers an altered representation to Ideation. Ideation at the same time has adjusted itself to anticipate the current, ongoing sheep behaviour of walking.

If the two images match, Ideation is 'happy' and Meaning is asserted. If the two images do not match, then depending upon the lack of match, there may be less Meaning as Ideation adjusts its hypothesis as to what the sheep is doing. If we fear it is not a sheep at all, but something we do not recognise, then we lose Meaning altogether, and have to search memory for something that corresponds in some way to the grey-white blob before us.

Behaviour is stored and delivered as changes of shape, i.e. as a series of static frames like the still frames that are used to construct an animated cartoon film. However, since a black sheep will walk with the same walk as a white sheep, and both must share 'sheep-walking behaviour', the common walk must be captured by a series of template frames (like outline shapes) and we will end up fitting the observed secondary qualities of the sheep-like object extracted from the sensory block to the next frame in the series of motion templates. If the combination works, and anticipated behaviour matches detected behaviour then Meaning is asserted.)

## Behaviour is a Stimulus-Response pairing

Stimulus from an adjacent cluster, mid-behaviour, must be possible.

Is it sufficient to have a 'pixel image' break the bounds of the cluster it belongs to? If that occurs is there wiring[16] to the adjacent cluster for 'collision alert'? Is this the only kind of behaviour stimulus we need? We perceive cause and effect as stimulus response, as correlations[17]. Thus yes: action not-at-a-distance is all we need (Action apparently at a distance like that between magnets or the effect of gravity can be learned (searchable) behaviours as opposed to built-in neuron-architectural triggered operations).

**Is Ideation layered or are cluster types interwoven?**

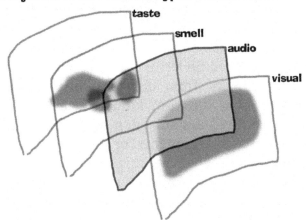

taste
smell
audio
visual

**(Not all cluster types need appear across all of Ideation)**

Figure 39. How are different senses organised to deliver qualia within the active region of Ideation?

---

16    Part of the house-keeping of Ideation.
17    A philosophical point.

So far the discussion has been mainly about the visual components of our understanding. Where does sound (or indeed any of the other senses) fit in?

We can experience sound in the same apparent three-dimensional realm as we do visible objects. Where in Ideation do qualia of sound come from, and how do they receive their content?

Often we associate the sounds we hear with a visible object, although sometimes the source of the sound is out of sight, or somewhere we cannot see (for instance behind us). At first blush we might posit a second private cinema screen in Ideation (Figure 39), closely parallel to the first, although in this case it is wrap-around, extending to the sides and above and below where visual qualia are generated—in fact it must manifest as a hollow sphere that encloses our apparent point of view, because sounds can be heard in all directions.

But there are two problems with this suggestion.

The first is that a plane (strictly speaking let's call it a surface) exists that is parallel to but closely behind the visual surface. Part of the motivation behind this is that we posited (in MIMH and elsewhere) that qualia that deliver content from different senses are themselves emitted from different kinds of neuron (or whatever other brain cell might be doing the donkey-work). There were reasoned arguments for this and even here it is not unreasonable when we think that the essentially two-dimensional 'pixel-cell' delivery of images is, intuitively going to require a different neuron micro-architecture (i.e. internally to a cluster) than an essentially one-dimensional audio signal.

Thus we take the view that audio and visual clusters are separate. Do they occupy separate cluster layers (a layer being a network that is connected exclusively to itself) or might the different clusters be tiled in some mosaic pattern?

It seems to me more likely that the two are indeed separate surfaces but which are cross-connected so that what we hear can be associated with what we see.

Indeed (invoking the subjectivist in us all) who has not had the experience of hearing a voice one recognises, in a gathering for instance, but assigning it to the back of the wrong head. Only when we see the face of our friend do we immediately relocate the source of the sound to its proper visual counterpart.

This apparent fluidity in the audio surface is also, of course, present in the visual surface, since when we turn our heads left or right, or look up or down, or indeed (slowly and carefully—don't try this at home!) perform a head stand; our visual field of view undergoes massive lateral, vertical and rotational changes.

This might be achieved by resetting and repopulating all the clusters of Ideation from scratch with each change (as if one were to drop off to sleep and open one's eyes afresh for any small change in orientation). But given the need of any creature always to be on the move and checking and rechecking the environment (for survival purposes), I suggest it is more likely that both visual and audio surfaces have massive shift and rotation capabilities built into inter-cluster connectivity; Any shift in any direction or change of orientation can happen in a single brain operation cycle[18].

---

18      I know the brain is not synchronous and the idea of an operation cycle is quintessentially a synchronous idea, but I wish to give an impression of the scale of the operation. Attributing a unit of time to a generic copy-your neighbour operation, one can envisage it taking several such cycles to pick features from the Sensory block, compare them to Memory, and load Ideation from scratch. All of which might be valuable survival time for a living creature. There may be a residual question of what is the order in which clusters are relieved of their contents (if all cells copy-paste all at once, they risk overwriting themselves at the same time they are being referenced. Although we could solve that problem in the internal architecture of the cluster. Alternatively we

Another factor that we must cater for (in fact we impose it as one of the key restrictions of our model brain, to be pseudo-conscious) is that if consciousness is delivered by a three-dimensional field of real-world gleeons (massive in number and sub-atomic in size as per MIMH)[19] then all the gleeons that contribute to the single unified feeling thing that makes each of us the thinking, experiencing thing that we are, those gleeons must be physically close enough to each other to interact and unify within the gleeon field that pervades all of space. In MIMH we postulated that this unification must be a little like coherent light in a laser, or some kind of resonance effect.

Whatever it is, for the gleeons to be unified, to create a single, feeling entity, they must be within some physical range of each other. I suggest that this range is of the order of magnitude of clusters[20]. I think, certainly, that the influence of one gleeon upon another does not extend to distances measured in many centimetres (or inches), otherwise you would only have to bump heads with someone to read their mind... Possibly the answer lies in gleeons' being borne the whole length and whole breadth of some neurons, and having a relatively small range of effectiveness beyond the cell wall of the neuron (or beyond whatever internal neuronal feature captures and mates them).

---

might look at the order in which Ideation normally picks cluster content from the Sensory block and Memory on 'first awareness'. As suggested later in the text, this might be a spiral from a central point of focus (or indeed include a good deal of parallelism, or combine several approaches). Nonetheless it does not look like an insoluble problem, but would seem to be more time-efficient to shift or rotate the whole of Ideation content, co-ordinated with body movement, when thought of in terms of this notional operational cycle , i.e. than compared to a full 'where on earth am I first awareness' reset.

19      I.e. when each of the gleeons is mated with a datum of content provided by a brain cell, and characteristic of that brain cell, the field of mated gleeons (i.e. for the duration of the mating, they contribute to qualia).

20      One might want to say less, to argue that it can extend hardly any further than a neuron—although some neurons may cross the brain, indeed extend across the length of the body.

The upshot is that we cannot build an arbitrary number of surfaces for various senses; thinking in these terms the surface would also need to be a single surface because to do otherwise would be to require a homunculus to make sense of any structure conveyed by the relative physical positions of the surfaces.

We cannot allow such a homunculus; if homunculus we must have, it can only be a collection of simple feelings; once we have constructed our brain-like conceptual engine to feed this notional feeling-only homunculus, we can remove him and leave a conceptual machine which we can reward or punish via the unexpressed content that our cut-down minimalist homunculus would have experienced.

Any separate surfaces we posit must therefore be intimately joined.

Returning to the question of the audio surface, we have introduced a new idea: that awareness is all-encompassing, coming at us from all directions, i.e. is wrap-around.

The *wrap-around* implies a spacial relation between the apparent point of view and the content so-viewed. But to do this is also to invoke a homunculus i.e. to do the viewing; any homunculus we introduce can only be the absolute minimum 'stuff' of experience; it can feel but it cannot process anything.

If we rely on a point of view at the centre of a hollow sphere then we have introduced space, and the need to interpret space. We cannot have that. All data processing, all understanding, implication and meaning(m) is done by the physical apparatus of the brain, what is left for consciousness is only the feeling of the content served up by the brain and the feeling that this content is adequate (Meaning(M)) from moment to moment.

So let us be careful, if we make the active surface in Ideation a hollow sphere then we must insist that consciousness subsists only in the surface itself, and not outside the surface or in any way separate from the surface[21].

That said, one question lingers: our sense of up and down; our sense of the correctness of seeing things the right way up. I suggest it is associated with Meaning being stronger when we impose on our world the directionality towards stability offered by the gravitational effect of the earth upon our bodies.

Our strong sense of the rightness of up and down is encoded by our brains to deliver a stronger sense of Meaning when Ideation organises itself in that particular directional way—and this directionality (or orientation) is related ultimately to the orientation of our bodies, what is stable for us in waking life, and to those senses we possess which exclusively report the internal state of our bodies (not least balance via the inner ear) and how those senses fit into the rest of the Ideation picture.

Put another way: our world view is relative to our view of our own bodies.

Given these new considerations about layers of clusters, let us revisit the idea (or problem) of the unseen

---

21    Talk of a hollow sphere does not have to be literal. Any closed surface that is topologically equivalent to a sphere would serve the purpose. We want only qualia-continuity in any direction. Indeed we might envisage our closed surface as having holes in it. How would we ever know? Perhaps we would know because there would be [literally] blind spots. We would not know what we cannot feel. Indeed we might question whether complete continuity in all directions is needed for a complete and continuous experience of the world. Might not a closed latticed surface work equally as well? Possibly yes. Does this affect our architecture, or our main point? Re. architecture: we would allow ourselves more processing space for supportive neuron functions. Re. proximity of layers: we do still need sounds and images to be able to co-exist on the surface of our inner cinema screen, meaning that sound qualia/gleeons must be capable of alignment, cheek-by-jowl, to visual qualia/gleeons, to appear to co-exist co-extensively in our experiential field. Thus, even if our 'closed' surface is a lattice, where the latticework exists, if there are visual clusters there **must be** audio clusters in close proximity. At first blush it seems visual clusters extend—or are active—over only a part of the closed surface, whereas we can perceive sounds from any direction at any time.

lamb behind the sheep (or the unseen fox running along the far side of the hedge).

We do not want to introduce some arbitrary number of cluster surfaces to account for all of the unseen but suspected or inferred presences in the green, hedge-enclosed field that we see through the window of our study-room.

First let us consider a non-existent lamb or non-existent fox. Suppose someone is standing behind me as I sit at my desk in my study. This person says, "Did you see that fox? It slipped through the bars of the gate, and behind the hedge."

I look up, I scrutinise the hedge as best I can (it is about one hundred metres away). I try to find evidence of a fox, or of anything moving behind the hedge. I see nothing but the hedge. What am I actually doing?

First, I retain the words, or at least the gist of them i.e. "fox behind hedge". Second the focus of my attention travels the hedge from left to right, trying to find fox-shapes (or some fragment of the expected shade of brown) peaking through. I cannot match any part of what I see in the direction of the hedge to the archetypal shape or colour I have in mind for my concept of fox.

How does this work? How can this work?

I speculate there is a fox behind the hedge. I place my imagined fox in my visual field. I add it as a suitable number of foxy-clusters[22] to Ideation, but then immediately re-fetch the visual data from the Sensory block, corresponding to that bit of hedge and see if I get any kind of a match. The fox is not visible, my speculation as to its [visible] presence is immediately defeated, and those foxy clusters are replaced by a boring patch of hedge.

---

22    Enough fox-component clusters to approximate to a real fox at the estimated distance, should one so appear.

My imagination[23] overlays my fox across some portion of the hedge, and briefly, ghost-like, I perceive it, then it is gone, corrected by apparent 'reality'.

The problem is, I do not see a flash of real fox, suddenly to be wiped out by reality. I might invent fox patterns which are keyed on strange gnarled features of the hedge. But the speculated fox, until real, is never real.

The imagined fox, in this scenario, is at best ghost-like. Am I to invent another surface, parallel to those that correspond to sensory data, which is a layer of speculation? Well, no. To do so would be to invite any number of layers for however deep my speculation goes. For instance, if I stand in front of a ten foot brick wall, and I am told there are fifty parallel walls of a similar height on the far side of it, do I spontaneously generate fifty wall bearing surfaces, one apparently behind another[24]?

If I want to keep my fox in the same layer as my active visual representation of the world, albeit fleetingly, I need it to be a real ghost, something suggested but not quite realised. I need it to be semi-transparent or mist-like. Indeed I would seek the same explanation of my ghost fox as I would an explanation of the sight of the green field and the sheep and the tree when seen through a thin mist.

How is mist possible, and to be understood, when incorporated into the visual surface?

Are we to tile clusters of mist and clusters of what lies through the mist? i.e. given the minuscule contribution to qualia from each cluster (the microscopic granularity of the contribution of each 'pixel'), a simple 50% tiling of mist and hedge would *appear* smooth.

Alternatively does the mist interfere with, overlay and corrupt pixel-level data within the cluster? Does mist

---

23     Whatever mechanism I might invent for that, perhaps a memory fetch-scale-and-load.
24     Which breaks the homunculus principle in any case.

corrupt cluster data, allowing only a partial rendering of our hedge, or our fox?

In the latter case, if cluster data is incomplete at least we have a built-in mechanism for matching as best we can whatever there is in the cluster, since if the FT-list is less than perfect for a fox, when we send that FT-list to Memory to find the best match for it, what returns might be a fox, or a dog.

Also, the mechanism for this (in terms of the operation of the brain/the mechanics of cluster management) will be easier to implement merely by allowing a cluster to load an FT-list and perform some simple [pixel]cell-wise combination, be it addition, or subtraction, a mask or a logical function, AND, OR, XOR etc. Such things are simply achieved.

However, meaning must be preserved for any number of (part-)visible objects combined in this way. So the pixel-wise associative links (unless we extend the model of the cluster to allow arbitrarily many links per pixel/cell) suggests we need to perform logical yes-no operations at pixel/cell level, which yield a single datum from one or other competing image, and alongside that datum (pixel/cell) we insert the associative link belonging to that cell in the original object (i.e. at that pixel in the object). Thus a cluster carries meaning of both (or as many as) objects or object-elements that have been merged into it, and in proportion to the degree of merger and representative of just those parts that survive the merger.[25]

Returning to the view through my study the window, and my friend who reports seeing a fox:

Alternatively, upon hearing the words, I merely look and wait for motion, alert to any change, whereupon I can do my fox-pattern matching thing, applying it now to a

---

25      We will not add layers. We will not tile clusters. We will tile the cells within each cluster. Also we could use 'outlines' or 'key features' as are used in behaviour clusters, when speculating or competing with data that comes directly from the Sensory block. Imagination uses behaviour templates.

specific region of disturbance in the pattern of the hedge.

All the time, I keep in mind (somewhere, I have yet to work out where), the gist of those words, "fox behind hedge," and so long as I am not distracted more urgently (by words such as, "the pub opened ten minutes ago") I keep scanning the hedge until I announce, "Nah, the sheep hasn't moved, and it would have noticed, believe me."[26]

We have the idea of the proximity (if not in some way co-extensive e.g. via a finely woven cloth of overlapping neural clusters) of visual and audio surfaces, and of a closed qualia-emitting surface, possibly a lattice[27][28].

We have other senses which we must incorporate into our grand qualia-generating engine. These other senses, such as taste, smell and pain, have localities which are peculiar to them but must have a proper place in our qualia-only world view.

In terms of the closed qualia-surface, some regions of

---

26    I may not be right, of course, but I have to cross the field to get to the pub, so...

27    Technically, mathematically, someone will say that a lattice is not a closed surface. That a lattice allows access between inside and outside. Well, my closed surface is the inside of a hollow sphere. My lattice is derived from that and the shorthand I am using to convey the gist of this arrangement is to coin the term 'closed lattice'. Still, there is a sense of something being 'viewed' from the inside, and this sense of a POV i.e. of a sidedness of the lattice (inside or outside) needs to be resisted. What we require of our closed lattice surface is that if you traverse it—i.e. shift the focus of attention—in any direction you return to your starting point, as would happen if you rotate the sum total of experience in a circle centered on the centre of the focus of attention.

28    It is also to be emphasized that the closed surface lattice does not have to be physically spherical. It might be crumpled and creased, even with what might look like folds. The physical space occupied by the qualia have no meaning to the qualia. Qualia only 'know' what the brain feeds them by way of datums. Nor is there any need for the closed surface lattice to be tied to any particular region of Ideation. The lattice may wander through Ideation, so long as there is continuity of the unified field of mated gleeons and the qualia which that mating produces.

this surface may be dedicated predominantly to e.g. taste and smell[29].

For us, as humans, it may not be possible to smell something as coming from any region other than the nose (even when we move our heads, if the content of Ideation shifts and rotates in synchronisation with our physical bodily movements, then the position of our nose in Ideation does not move at all).Taste is slightly different, since we can move our tongue, suck on a sweet, or lick an ice cream cone. But even the region of *the Surface* capable of generating tastes may be limited. If I lick a splodge of spilled ice cream off my arm, I do not place the taste on my arm; taste belongs to my tongue, and to wherever it can move *relative to my head* (Figure 39).

Parts of my body will also contribute to the content of the closed surface, although these will all be capable of much more positioning than the tongue. I can place a hand anywhere in the three-dimensional space around me; my feet in many places, my lower back not so many (I don't do yoga). But I can have a pain anywhere in my body, which may be experienced in any direction and at a variety of distances from my apparent point of view (although here I must be careful with words, since I do not allow the residual feeling-only homunculus a literal point of view, perhaps 'axis of experience' is better).

Those senses that can give rise to feelings from the skin or from inside the body must have corresponding qualia-generating clusters in Ideation. Possibly, given that some parts of the body (the hands) can move to anywhere relative to the axis of experience, such body-senses can be expressed anywhere across the closed surface lattice— even where nothing can be seen, e.g. if I place my hand behind my head and tug my hair at the back.

---

29      Thus the closed surface lattice might be pinned at those regions to specific regions of Ideation, or limited in the degree to which the lattice may wander in Ideation i.e. to maintain the connection between e.g. the neural clusters that can deliver qualia of smell, and those regions of the closed surface lattice that do deliver qualia of smell.

(Remember a constraint we have placed on qualia generation is that among secondary qualities, all flavours for a particular sense (the range of colours for light, the range of tones for sound) are delivered by one kind of neuron (or whatever brain cell) which is limited to producing the flavours of qualia that belong to that sense. We have not proposed a general purpose generate-any-feeling neuron. Whether this is a necessary consequence of the essential nature of different kinds of neuron, or a pragmatic consequence of where neurons are functionally located, may not matter, since different sensory processes would seem to require that Ideation clusters with different internal neural arrangements (e.g. 2-D visual as against 1-D audio) are distributed across the Surface.)

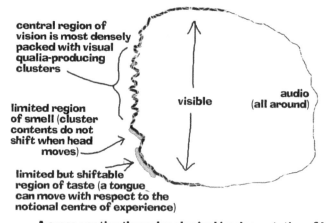

central region of vision is most densely packed with visual qualia-producing clusters

limited region of smell (cluster contents do not shift when head moves)

limited but shiftable region of taste (a tongue can move with respect to the notional centre of experience)

visible

audio (all around)

A cross-section through a physical implementation of Ideation and through the closed surface lattice, illustrating where qualia of four different kinds may be generated.

Figure 40. A cross-section of our closed surface lattice.

Figure 40 shows what a cross-section of our closed surface lattice might look like in terms of Ideation clusters that are able to generate qualia of sound, vision, taste and smell.

It may meander through the brain substrate[30] and

---

30    Its location might be fixed and static, or it may move in the sense that different clusters become active as focus and content within Ideation

be more or less densely packed by Ideation clusters and especially densely packed in the region we think of as the visual region which is richest with information (remembering that focus of attention as per MIMH follows the densest cluster activity, not necessarily the densest cluster packing—when you scratch that itch in the middle of your back you can see nothing of the location but that is where you focus your attention).

We are proposing an Ideation space which gives rise to and supports an active qualia-bearing surface where both the density of qualia-bearing clusters and the intensity of activity in different groups of clusters vary from one moment to the next depending, respectively, on richness of data and focus of attention.

However, we perceive the world as a uniformly distributed arrangement of objects and materials. If I focus for a few seconds on a particular word on this page, that word does not grow in size simply because it is now at the centre of my visual field (where there is more detailed information available to me about it, as well as, being the focus of attention (as our model would have it) its associative links and other cluster activity is maximised).

What is missing is some sense of scaling.

Should we abandon the idea that some regions of the surface are more densely packed with qualia-bearing clusters than another? Which is to say that clusters of any one kind would instead be evenly distributed at some density representative of the fractional angle of the arc of the world view which a particular cluster represents (albeit intermingled with qualia bearing clusters of other kinds), Figure 41.

---

change and as a result the active areas that define the lattice move, in effect moving the lattice. At this point in the development of the model neither option is ruled in or out.

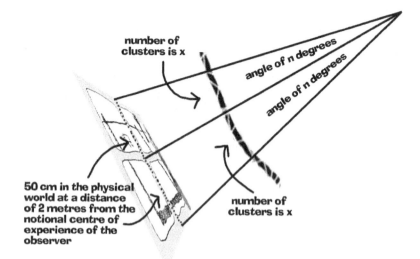

Figure 41. Does each qualia-bearing cluster represent the same angle of the inner (spherical) cinema screen of our experience? I.e. do any given number of clusters 'x', always represent the same angular portion 'n' of the physical world when our view of the physical world is thought of as projected onto the inside surface of a sphere?

If 'number of clusters' translates directly to 'angle of the world viewed', then we will require the same density of visual clusters at the edge of the visual region as we have at the centre of the visual region, but those clusters at the edge are less active qualia-producers (because focus is at the centre of the visual region, and detail at the centre is better defined). However, if fewer qualia are produced, then the experience is less dense and on the equal-angle for equal-cluster-number principle above, the edges of the visual field would represent a smaller portion of the world view, and the world would appear to distort as we moved eyes and head.

This would happen because a mainstay of our theory of perception is that there can be no homunculus. But if we rely on cluster density separately from qualia density then we need a homunculus to know about, and process the fact that, some clusters are inactive when they are at the edge of the visual region (and yet they would still be providing spacial information).

So we cannot rely on the idea of equal cluster numbers for equal angle-of-view in the world. And by the same token we cannot rely on the idea of equal qualia numbers for equal angle-of-view in the world and what we are forced to do is to find a way of incorporating some sense of space, size, distance etc.—in fact what elsewhere we have referred to as *primary qualities*—into experience.

At the same time we *could* envisage the same density of clusters across the whole visual region and allow some peripheral clusters to be inactive (i.e. not all of them produce qualia) in order to serve as a reservoir of pre-loaded clusters for when the head of the observer turns left or right or up or down (or the eyes move left or right etc.) and cluster contents are shifted (in the opposite direction) to keep whatever is at the focal point of the retina also at the centre of the visual region of The Surface (for speedily checking expected against actual). This might prove more efficient than fetching and loading the extra detail required by the focal clusters as focus changes.

What would be most efficient for Nature and what would Occam's Razor suggest? It is trade-off between cluster count (a physical resource, measured in protein and carbohydrate) versus a time factor (measured in milliseconds). In terms of evolutionary advantage plausibly any creature, predator or prey, would benefit from speed, favouring additional clusters which are pre-loaded. In terms of design, what is simplest? Possibly also pre-loading, since all clusters then operate in the same way, and we rely on the principle of focus of attention to determine how intense qualia production is in any region of The Surface.

And yet the clusters loaded at the periphery of vision are tested against less rich data from the visual field and more likely to be mistaken, and unreliable. And simply saying that qualia could be generated in a consistent density but are not, or have quiescent content, does not account for why the *experience* of the periphery of our vision is less detailed (or intense) than at the centre.

Above, we have no satisfactory theory as to how to explain or implement high resolution experience in specific parts of the field of view while maintaining homogeneity.

But perhaps topology can save us, Figure 42.

In Figure 42, the rules of topology i.e. of placing one item with respect to another, require that clusters A, B, C, D, E and F deliver higher resolution than clusters P, Q and R. There is nothing to interpret, no homunculus needed, simple geometry demands the outcome we are looking for.

**Cross section, front-to-rear, through the Surface**

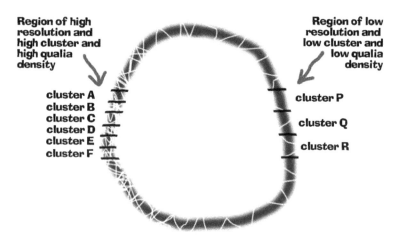

**Region of high resolution and high cluster and high qualia density**

cluster A
cluster B
cluster C
cluster D
cluster E
cluster F

**Region of low resolution and low cluster and low qualia density**

cluster P

cluster Q

cluster R

Figure 42. Cluster A is above cluster B, yet both clusters A and B are directly to the left of cluster P (the cross section is of the hollow sphere of the Surface). Topology requires that A, B, C, D, E, and F are more densely packed than P, Q and R, and so A, B, C, D, E, and F necessarily support a higher resolution representation of the world.

We turn then to the question of primary qualities and whether they are experienced through primary quality qualia (extension, hardness and so on) or are conveyed through secondary qualities (colours, sounds etc.), or even through behaviours (which we have so far mooted as changes in secondary qualities).

Since we only ever infer the primary qualities of things and stuffs in the world through our perception of the secondary qualities that we attribute to those things and stuffs, how do we make those inferences?

In part the answer is going to be by extending our examination of secondary qualities to the whole panoply of sensory perceptions that we enjoy, including sensations gathered from the skin, and from musculature (and from internal organs etc.), and how we act and interact with the physical world, and our awareness of our bodies in, and as part of, the physical world.


Mention of how we interact with the physical world requires some account of the self. What it is, how we learn about it, and how we maintain and refine our sense of it.

How is our sense of self united? By pain or by observing things done to it, and by it, and learning the extent of, and giving shape to what is part of it and what is other to it.

As it explores and experiments, its fingers will give it small scale distance, arms [literally] reaching distance and legs crawling distance—on a scale of at least several metres.

It can learn that things appear smaller or bigger according to distance; but how is distance encoded?

Are we going to have to introduce a quale for distance—such and such *feels* a long way away? Because doing so is something of a cheat. We can't simply bestow qualia on any cognitive problem we encounter, not least because it reintroduces the need for a homunculus to make sense of all these all-too-convenient sensations.

Flexing a finger, or an arm, however, has a sensation associated with it. As does crawling (or walking), especially when one encounters a hard object, meeting resistance, possibly pain, and possibly also noise.

Thinking about distance, and the trajectory of a small child through the world, much of what it might perceive will involve collisions, and fallings down, and here might be our entrée to capturing the concept of distance, and extension depth-wise, in space.

When an object is knocked over, if it remains intact, its vertical height will be rendered horizontal, with some foreshortening in appearance. If observed from any distance, the object that has been knocked over could be said to display the behaviour of falling, meaning its shape changes in a characteristic way, and it can in turn stimulate the behaviour of some nearby object if the two are seen to collide (I'm thinking dominoes here).

We could thus attribute three dimensional distance in a direction-of-travel away from an observer to a behaviour of a two dimensional object, as it might be perceived without any depth.

Suppose we simply assert that depth in space is measured in terms of falling-down distance sans-collision, as available visually via two-dimensional shape behaviour. Falling-down distance could be available at a variety of scales: finger-size, arm-size, walking-size, and perhaps not difficult to extrapolate to trees and other large and distant objects. But in encapsulating depth by behaviour, we cannot appreciate depth unless we play out that behaviour. How does our non-homunculean viewer appreciate such depth unless something falls over or the non-homunculus pictures it as falling over. All of which takes time. And if our non-homunculean observer needs to play something forward in imagination, will that observer not need its own memory to compare what might be, with what is?

Behaviour (as per Memory object, cluster etc. behaviour) may help the non-homunculus anticipate and confirm the way the world is. Superimposing behaviours is intrinsic to cluster operation (and the comparison process itself is not rendered as qualia). Indeed the non-homunculus may observe behaviour play out in imagination, but this is the doing of the brain, because the brain does everything at this stage[31]. Our non-homunculus is merely a collection of qualia.

Could we express depth by incorporating behaviour into the current/present/now Ideation clusters as one might the ghost of the fox behind the hedge, or a mist?

That option also would not appear to be available to us since it would require our non-homunculus to interpret the combined 'now' and 'maybe soon' images.

Perhaps depth could be interpreted in terms of the amount of effort that the body would need to expend (muscles, breath, tiredness—all felt things) in order to traverse some distance. The plant pot on the window sill is within easy reach. The gate to the field is a laborious walk away. And yet, still, these are implications and would need to be interpreted by the non-homunculus, turning him or her back into a fully equipped homunculus of the fairground kind.

Consider this: I want to fetch a jar from the far corner of a corner kitchen cupboard. What I have in mind is one of those cupboards where you have to stick your head inside to take a look, work out where the jar is, and then reach in blindly, estimating where your hand is, in space, inside the cupboard and hopefully land your fingers on the jar without knocking it, or anything else, over.

What is going on in your conscious mind that enables you to do that? How do you keep and use the sense of space required to perform the task?

---

31    MIMH maintains that consciousness plays a causal role in brain activity in order to have achieved evolutionary advantage and survive as a feature, but causation is strictly limited and does not apply in this scenario.

At times, the jam jar may not even fall within the prospective scope of the visual region of Ideation (so there can be no playing-out of visual behaviours).

The jam jar is, necessarily, within the scope of the sensations region of Ideation that your hand and arm can cause to emit qualia (i.e. give rise to feelings of some kind). What is it about the secondary qualities that arise from arm and hand that support a meaningful three-dimensional model in not only the hand and arm but also of where the jar is located?

What secondary qualities are available to us? From the skin we have hot and cold, pressure, pain, tautness, itching, goosebumps. From within the arm: muscular tension, pain, swelling, throbbing (of heart beat in arteries), trembling.

When I put my arm into the cupboard how do I know where it is at any one time? Experience tells me. And practice. I can move my arm as I wish, reliably and accurately. Although I cannot see the jar, I can imagine it (suggesting that maybe the visual region of Ideation actually extends across the whole of The Surface. If so we can suggest that only where data from the retina arrives for comparison can visually verified qualia be emitted, making emissions dense at the centre of retina and less dense, less intense and impression-only elsewhere—especially behind the head, except what one can imagine).

I can imagine my arm, and hand as they move unobserved. And yet where does the sense of depth come from? Is there, at all times, superimposed upon our non-homunculus field of qualia a simple distinction of things within reach or range of our bodies, or outside reach?

A sense of what can be felt (a region of space, depth-wise), and what cannot be felt; a region into which our body might extend. But: how is this felt? Is it a learned possible body space, which in conjunction with skin-feeling and muscle feeling we know to be empty; we

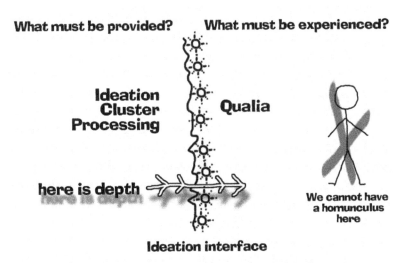

Figure 43. How is depth conveyed to the sum total of our perception? Qualia in The Surface cannot hold beliefs such as "X is above Y" or "Z is 3D"

feel the extent to which the body might occupy in any direction—yet that needs an understanding of 3D space, especially depth.

Let us approach the question from a different angle.

Part of what we are about in this text is devising a conceptual machine: a device in silicon or software which, when operating, is capable of juggling with ideas, and coming up with new ideas and with theories. Our approach to the problem of designing such a machine has been to argue: such a machine juggles with ideas in a way that is not dissimilar from the way we humans juggle with ideas. Except (we posit) such a machine will not be conscious, not least because *Why should it?* In order for it not to be conscious we draw on the theory of consciousness in MIMH and observe that all and only consciousness adds to the human machine is some slight evolutionary advantage over an otherwise similar brain-driven creature. The theory of MIMH suggests that consciousness achieves no more and no less than the sum total of the qualia that constitute it, with a small causal side-effect, but distinctly without performing any processing or analysis itself—which would defeat the analysis in MIMH of what consciousness is, since 'processing or analysis' would beg the question and introduce a fully fleshed homunculus.

Part of what we need to present in terms of qualia is depth. How can we convey depth without requiring any processing after all our data is represented as qualia?

We have suggested before now that depth may be encapsulated implicitly in behaviour—in what can be thought of as *falling down* behaviour.

We can treat behaviour simply as a series of changes to perceptual data. When a toddler falls over, the ground that was some distance from it, moves towards it, becoming bigger (i.e. closer) in a certain characteristic way. Similarly when it observes dominoes fall, each displays a certain falling behaviour which involves the perceived shape of them changing (they rotate around their bottom edge and the top edge is foreshortened as they fall, say, away from the observer).

However, behaviour involves time. Behaviour plays out over time. Even if we call upon imagination to play out what might happen we are not appreciating depth directly and in the moment. We are not perceiving depth instantly, when surely we must?

We might recall from MIMH and the Lock Step model that the time window of active perception is not confined to an infinitesimally short instant of time. Rather, we allow for some drag in the ribbon of consciousness, which translates to limited gleeon (and qualia) longevity and overlap and therefore some sense of continuity of the unity of the perceiving being.

However, this brief time overlap allowance hardly seems enough to convey the persuasive strength we have of our feeling of depth in the world, and perhaps ignores a more serious problem: How are we entitled even to a two dimensional arrangement of qualia? Where do these two dimensions come from if they are not provided by a homunculus viewing the patchwork quilt of visual qualia?

There are some sensations we experience which have no particular spacial component: both rage and love are all-consuming. They engulf us; they are simply everywhere inside our conscious mind; they lack any dimensionality; let us say they have zero dimensionality. Sound is different. We often think of it as one-dimensional—it is a series of pitches. However, usually, we perceive it as coming from some particular direction or other. In that sense it has both an angle of elevation and an angle of rotation with respect to the way we are

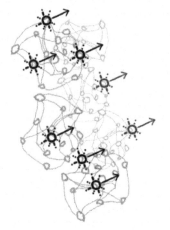

Qualia have directionality and line up because the underlying gleeons line up regardless of the orientation of the neuronal structures that give rise to them

Locally qualia line up parallel to one another but on a larger scale they define the inside of a closed surface, and all face inwards

**A section of the Surface in Ideation**

Figure 44. Gleeons are directional and tend to line up. Qualia are directional and tend always to assume one direction wrt The Surface, based on its being closed, and therefore having a slight energy advantage one way rather than another (like flocks of geese).

facing. Or, put another way, a sound will seem to originate from some location which we could map to The Surface. Sound, though one-dimensional in its nature, is two- (if not three-) dimensional as we perceive it.

Our visual field is more obviously two-dimensional. A splash of red may be left, right, above, or below a splash of yellow...

And yet this is not the worst of it since we have constructed The Surface as a closed entity which we populated with qualia as viewed from the inside.

How is it that consciousness, if it resides only in (the qualia of) The Surface is viewed from the inside out and not the outside in? Where does this directionality come from? And how do gleeons and qualia even support it? Are we to imagine that gleeon/qualia are directional and all point inwards towards the centre of the volume occupied by The Surface?

This is hard to digest, since we might reasonably expect clusters of neurons in Ideation to be orientated in many different ad hoc ways. Surely we are not going to require that they line up to form an orderly cinema screen? For one thing, I have no doubt that any such anatomical feature instantiated in the brain would have been spotted by the ancient Greeks, if not the Romans.

It may be fair to say, though, that gleeons align locally, and qualia are directional and the sensation of each is orthogonal to the alignment of gleeons (such so called Left hand and Right Hand rules are known in physics for electric and magnetic fields), and that the slight concave curvature of the Surface favours qualia directionality one way rather than another (i.e. inwardly).

This does not relieve us of the burden of explaining how we perceive two dimensions. If qualia exist only in The Surface, how *do* we perceive two dimensions?

What I'm getting at is this: Rage is, for the perceiver, pure and simple and universal. It engulfs everything that they are as a perceiving thing. It has no dimensionality. It transcends dimensionality. The qualia of rage is simple, total, and unifying.

Suppose the qualia of red were the same. Imagine

being engulfed in redness. The only thing in your mind, that fills your mind and, for all you know, fills the universe is the colour red. Surely that must be the purest qualia of red there is?

Now we replace the colour red with blue. But since you have no memory (all you are able to do is perceive a single qualia), for all you know the whole universe has always been blue[32].

Suppose instead we divide your perceived world 50:50 red and blue. The two qualia exist side by side, each occupying half an infinity. Is one to the left of the other, or vice versa? Is one above the other, or vice versa? Is one ahead or behind, or do they lie on a strange diagonal drawn across your universe?

What is your viewpoint—how can you even establish a viewpoint—in order to answer the question? Surely your viewpoint, since these are qualia, and these are the things of which perception are made up, *is* the qualia?

How do you have a view of them when they are both the thing viewed and the thing doing the viewing?

When we think of a region of the brain producing qualia, we can think of that region giving rise to feeling (sensation, percept or whatever), and we can imagine a set of perceptions that might be present in that region and, in effect, we (as outside observer, experimenter and contemplator) might read and interpret the content of that region, and think of it as having data projected onto it. But the region is doing more than offering a private screening of qualia to the individual whose brain we are peering into.

The key is that the qualia are not just the sensory data being viewed [perceived] but also doing the viewing [perceiving] of them.

And while rage appears to be essentially

---

32    Even if there is a slow transition, without memory there is no knowledge of change, and therefore no knowledge of the passage of time.

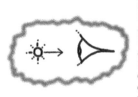

**a quale is
both
its own observer
and
its own content
and is
intrinsically
directional
content
to
observer**

Figure 45. A quale is both its own observer and its own content,
and is intrinsically directional: content-to-observer.

omnidirectional[33], it would seem that qualia of sound and
image are not.

If a quale encapsulates a sense of direction, we have to
ask what kind of dimensional (qualia/perception) space
does it express its directional vector in?

Jumping ahead: it does not strike me as very
satisfactory to suggest a three dimensional space, and
then go on to suggest that the qualia all point inwards
toward the centre of the physical real-world space at
the centre of The Surface, because that looks very much
like we have invented a homunculus to view the cinema
screen of the inner life of the brain.

Meaning: we have explained nothing. We have no
handle on what it is to perceive either two or three
dimensions.

Anticipating this, at least some improvement might
be had (and at the same time remove any need for The
Surface to have any correlative shape whatsoever with

---

33    Rage could be unidirectional but, being induced hormonally in the
brain, it might only ever affect The Surface in its totality, or not at all.

the perceived world, other than topology) by pointing out that each qualia has its viewpoint integral to it, albeit directional.

Taking this line, two dimensional space is perceived directly. However, any knowledge or belief that **it** is called two-dimensional, or has thus-and-such properties since it is two-dimensional, are all products of the brain which must be perceived as content (being mathematical theories that we recall, or hear about, or whatever) if any of it is to be 'understood' at all. All we perceive is that this red splash is next to the blue splash.

Given this arrangement, and supposing it is satisfactory, at least for the time being, where does that leave us with regard to the third dimension, depth?

If we have two dimensions[34], surely we can infer a third dimension?

Well, no. We cannot.

Were we to infer a third dimension we would be inventing a homunculus where so far we have only raw perception. We still need a mechanism to deliver depth (And using short time intervals and short-lived behaviour is not very convincing).

One temptation (and it seems to me at first blush, a cheat) might be to suggest that we perceive depth: to simply assert that there are qualia for depth.

When I place my hand in a cupboard and reach blindly for a jar of peanut butter in the far corner I am using what is called *proprioception*. This is a sense of where some part of my body is as a result of muscle tension, joint angle, and so on, as relayed from neurons throughout my body. I am able to judge where my hand is in relation to how I imagine some part of the world which, for whatever reason, is obscured from me.

---

34    Indeed if we simply have direction in 3D space.

Here I am using two methods of conceiving depth: skeleto-muscular and (memory of or imagination of) the world as perceived through the eyes.

No doubt all the senses played a part in building up my understanding of depth as I explored the world from the cradle onwards, but not even proprioception is delivering pure depth perception. It is a combination of perceptual components from which depth is inferred. The brain arrives at some inference of depth, generating some expectation of where the peanut butter is in relation to where the fingers are, and this wholly imagined scene (without any visual reinforcement) captures and conveys some element of depth, both usefully to further brain processing and informationally to perception. But how does perception receive and understand depth information through its two-dimensional perceptual field?

We are back to square one. How do we encapsulate depth if we cannot use behaviour because behaviour depends on time while depth is perceived without delay?

Let us go back even further and recall that the idea behind the Lock Step model of consciousness is that the seat of consciousness is where how the brain expects the world to be is compared with evidence from the senses.

Thus it is the brain that constructs a model of the world, and can include whatever time-dependent or behaviour-dependent aspects seem appropriate but only the product of that endeavour, where it matches input from the senses, is actually perceived.

Depth need not be perceived at all.

If the expectation constructed by the brain correctly attributes three-dimensional elements, then the two-dimensional impression of that three-dimensional world which the brain generates will be in good agreement with the two-dimensional evidence from the senses, which is all that is in fact needed, for two reasons:

First, we have already posited a qualia of Meaning(M) which is generated when a sufficiency of associations are present in the neural clusters of Ideation. If our generated image of a sheep on a hillside is consistent with all that we know about sheep and hillsides and is a good match for the available sensory evidence, then we will have that special feeling of confidence that goes with knowledge: "I can see for myself it's a sheep. I know it's a sheep. What else could it be?" The physical brain does the processing and the qualia of the mind do no more than provide awareness as to the outcome of the operation.

Second, while we may form an impression of the hillside, and we (our minds) feel confident that our brains have correctly identified what is in front of us, our brains will focus first on this element, then on some other element in the scene. For each element that gains the focus of attention, all (or many of) its associations are briefly loaded into Ideation[35] and those associations which are of special interest (e.g. by sharing the greatest number of associative links with this particular element, say, the sheep) can not only be supplied to clusters that contribute to The Surface (for e.g. the smell, touch, sound etc. as well as the observer's emotional reaction to a sheep) which will make the sheep feel more real, but also, when focus of attention settles on the sheep, expected behaviours can start to be played out, including those that illustrate size and distance.

Which is all to say, we do not need to look for depth in the qualia of The Surface. Depth is a given because the brain has successfully generated a match for incoming data, and this is reflected by a strong feeling of confidence associated with the elements in the scene which the brain has chosen to isolate and present in Ideation. Thereafter, any element in the scene receiving focus is (in a slower and

---

35    At the focus of attention in The Surface there is a far greater density of Ideation clusters.

more deliberate way) fully loaded into Ideation and all the consequence of that element's existence—in sensory and memory terms—are available to The Surface, including verbal rationalisations and memories of 3D perspective drawing at school (if you were lucky enough to do that), and even being reminded of the effort and pain that will come your way if you go through that gate and walk up the hill.

Who has not looked at an umbrella and immediately felt a twinge of wetness down their back?

## Time

The Surface of qualia does not understand time; our non-homunculean is no more than the sum of what it feels.

Allowing the Surface to 'understand' time would be like allowing it to 'understand' the third dimension—it would become a fully fledged homunculus and a meaning processor in its own right, and our quest for a brain-ish, thinking machine, fails, falling short of its goal.

Qualia are short lived, as are the gleeons that give rise to them. Each gleeon will exist for approximately as long[36] as the micro quale it gives rise to. Mostly this will be a small fraction of a second although maybe one or two might last as long as second[37].

Nonetheless, the concept of time is not available to them.

Even the 'observation' that qualia come and go is an observation, made by me as a homunculus. Such observations are not available to the Surface. The Surface cannot step outside itself and see itself change; we would get question-beggingly into a circle.

If time is not given by a feeling—if there are no qualia for time, per se—time, like extension that provides the

---

36      Shortly longer, as per the mechanism in MIMH
37      I.e. as an indicator of the time scales we are dealing with.

3$^{rd}$ dimensional in space, must be learned and carried by some composite of other, feel-able properties[38].

The obvious candidates in our model that might together capture time are behaviour and Meaning.

Behaviour captures a series of changes in any property and Meaning can endorse an anticipated change when it is borne out.

Let me be bold and globally generalise something we suspect to be true, at least in part, and locally:

We are always in a state of anticipating what will happen next. When what we expect to happen happens we are rewarded with a burst of Meaning.

This means that in Ideation, all the time, we are playing out the next thing that we expect to happen (we are always trying to load the next behaviour of a thing, even when there is no associated behaviour, we will be hard-wired to try).

Consequently, all the time, across the whole of the Surface, the most likely behaviour[39] of every thing or stuff which has been recognised, is superimposed on the confirmed present, like a thing imagined, or in mist[40].

The transition to the next behavioural state of that thing or stuff is verified, and a burst of Meaning accompanies it. Time is manifest only as a pair of co-extensive qualia: a ghostly anticipation that lacks Meaning (in our visual or whatever field), plus a substantive, Meaning-blessed quale that is the materialisation of the ghost of a moment before.

Note however that the transition is not perceived.

There is no homunculus to perceive any transition. There is no memory of there being first one feeling then another. Rather the pre-change qualia and the post-change

---

38    And only ever in the ongoing 'now' which makes the problem worse. The question of what time is, is an old hoor anyway.

39    I.e. the next frame in the series of frames that constitute behaviour.

40    It is a behaviour, after all, and that was how we envisaged behaviours as being instantiated.

qualia share a space. Many, many gleeons contribute to a single perceivable quale, and these gleeons and the micro qualia they produce can and do intermingle as two clouds or mists might intermingle.

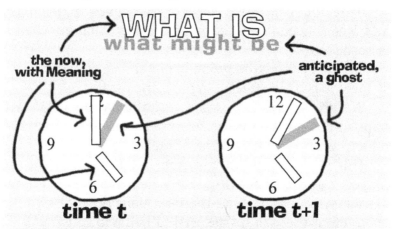

The Surface cannot sense the passage of time but at any instant in time it senses the ghost of the future which provides continuity (qualia persist in time) but of course can mean nothing beyond that.

Figure 46. The Surface cannot sense (detect) time, has no sense (feeling) of time, and has no understanding of time. The brain may rationalize about time, in words, but words are merely sounds accompanied by concepts which, to the Surface, are as ghostly as the anticipated future.

For the Surface, time does not exist. For the Surface all that exists are a confirmed reality, which is endorsed by Meaning, and an unconfirmed reality which lacks the same substance and lacks the same endorsement. Figure 46.

Time is the ghost of the next thing that *might* happen.

The ghost of the next frame of behaviour is continually re-presented for every object and for every sense in the surface (even the non-moving and never-known-to-move objects) and this, in conjunction with the cogitations acquired when objects of interest receive focus of attention, delivers the overall and convincing impression of a tangible three-dimensional space.

# 10. Work Ethic

We have set up a machine that operates a work cycle of:

Ideation fetches cluster data from the Sensory block and requests the cleaned-up version of the cluster data from Memory. Memory supplies its best matching thing or stuff to the cluster data, including all the associative links for that thing or stuff. Ideation loads the cluster data for the thing or stuff that Memory has provided into the Surface, and if the context provided by all the associative links (to Memory and to other clusters in Ideation) are sufficient to suggest that what has been fetched from Memory is veridical, then a quale of Meaning is generated.

When this cycle repeats we have a machine that (given sufficient content in Memory) can observe the world and in some sense make sense of it.

We have hinted that the Sensory block might be a generic pattern matching region of our brain-ish device. It might well be a (relatively simple) convolutional neural network (CNN). This, I think, would work.

Our brain-ish machine at this stage is completely passive in its operation (and who knows where it collected its repertoire of memories from).

If something new appears in the field of view, our machine can learn to recognise it, and lay down some memory for it, even learn any behaviours associated with the new thing (behaviours being cascades of clusters which can be addressed in Memory to arrive one after another, in sequence).

But our machine cannot come to understand depth

unless it has some agency and is able to do things in the world, even if only to wave a single two-clawed limb across its field of vision.

So we gift it limbs so that it might move and interact with the world, and of course with the limbs we gift it senses that are its equivalent to 'muscle flexing effort' and 'muscle tension' and senses of touch (each of these senses generating their own qualia which are generated, as per Figure 40 across areas of The Surface).

We do all this and our brain-ish machine in its sense-laden robotic fabrication sits and does nothing...

Why would it *do* anything?

It is lacking, as they say, motive and means (even though, I feel, I have given it opportunity).

Our brain-ish device lacks motive because we have not endowed it with either carrot or stick to do anything. Our brain-ish machine performs perfectly well up to and including the operation of The Surface, but our brain-ish machine is not flesh and blood; its Surface does not generate qualia, and it can have no experience of pain or pleasure and the motivations which accompany those two sensations.

(In fact we have probably forgotten to wire in pathways for pain or pleasure.)

We need to implement some basic penalty and reward mechanism, if only to get it to explore the world and learn[1].


## Generating choice and taking actions

Actions lie in Ideation / the Surface where we *follow* associations - so the Brain-ish thing, lets call him Steel, needs not merely to follow the most active associations

---

1        I am not talking here about morality. At this stage morality is entirely other from basic data-gathering, which is more akin to an ethically unaware toddler exploring the world.

but to follow the most active associations that equally provide the greatest reward. Therefore a measure of penalty or reward need to be part of any behaviour (and each Meaning calculation needs to fetch the sum total of penalty-rewards historically associated with a series of behaviours for those things linked to).

This is something of a computational overhead (it lacks the convenience of merely requesting an FT-list) but it is obviously fairly easily doable in the architecture we have set up.

That is motive.

As for means, we need to be able to control and monitor mechanical behaviour (arm and leg motion), and this too we can do through behaviours.

We can treat some behaviours as special, as 'belonging to the brain-ish device'. Special behaviours are ones that the brain-ish device can play out, can make happen, in its own limbs. When a special behaviour plays out in the Surface, the limbs of the brain-ish device are arranged to operate[2].

Things and stuffs which are not part of the self are merely observed. Things and stuffs that are part of the self can be activated (in the case of limbs).

Reward is implemented by making it more likely that one set of behaviours is chosen over another. Penalty is implemented by making it more likely that one set of behaviours is rejected in preference to some (any) other.

There is still the question, given an initial state of quiet quiescence: why should the brain-ish device do anything at all? Why make a first move?

We will have to introduce constant stimulation, or perturbation, which results in there always being activity in the Surface. This might be like a nervous tic, but it must at the same time be under full brain-ish control (how can

---

2       As best they can. the operation of complex cantilevered armatures and the like, may have to be learnt.

it learn what it cannot control; how can it be stimulated to do anything if it is not already doing something, itself?)

It is not enough that it is always searching for meaning (associative link chasing) because that does not necessitate taking any action.

We need to pre-program memory with a simple physical task that has a high reward, which it has the possibility of un-learning later.

The task must be harmless, or self limiting. For instance the action might be to extend its arm and wave its hand, but with a strict penalty (and 'stop playing out this behaviour') if a collision detector detects a collision.

We started this chapter by giving our device a static work cycle, and are moving towards what might be called an action cycle.

With movable limbs we have some prospect of the machine's picking up the sensory cues for physical, mechanical reach, which is necessary for it to understand the third dimension. And it has a mechanism, via Memory, of laying down and playing back behaviours, which will endow it with some sense of time (at least in respect of the world as it 'perceives' it).

We have looked at how we might stimulate it to its first action, whereafter we hope it might keep going, since that is what the Surface, being an instantiation of the Lock Step model is designed to do—to chase maximum meaning[3].

We have only hinted at conceptual thinking, which the brain-ish device in its current configuration might or might not be able to achieve. But our hint was that conceptual thinking, like the vagueness of an imagined fox, or of the sense-specific template that comprises each

---

3        i.e. maximum meaning in the form of maximum associative connectivity, but now factoring reward and penalty into the calculation of 'maximum'.

frame in a pattern of behaviour, or our vague distant 24x24 pixelated cat face, is some kind of Key Feature place-holder element, with many associations.

Certainly a great boon to conceptual thinking is the spoken (or thought or written) word.

And language is what we must look at next.

# 11. Language, Truth and Mr. Logic

We have already suggested that words might be associated with objects or tacked onto objects like an augmented reality display. Conceivably we might employ the whole of a large language model (LLM) artificial neural network, transformer and all, to provide the language component of our brain-ish device. I do not doubt it could be done. But it would undermine our purpose.

Not only do LLMs generate false statements (so-called hallucinations) but they do not understand anything (being neither conscious nor pseudo-conscious[1]), and so cannot align the material they spew out, or actions they cause to happen, to have any intrinsic moral dimension.

LLMs lie and they don't care!

Our brain-ish device must have language[2] but how, if we are not to rediscover and repeat the questionable benefits of LLMs?

Two approaches come to mind which, I suggest, might reasonably be rolled into one[3].

Let me just comment that LLMs are brute force calculating devices. They examine all the sentences of a language that they have access to, and compute (perhaps with some modicum of pattern recognition[4]) what is likely to be the next word. They run on computational processors

---

1    Being pseudo-conscious is of course the claim to fame of our brain-ish device.

2    We will want it to be able to reason linguistically and talk to us—and do so truthfully, of course.

3    Possibly with the blessing of philosopher and linguist Noam Chomsky, although what he would make of the project of this text, I would not dare to suppose.

4    The transformer bit.

that merely simulate the already over-simplified approximation to a neuron known as a perceptron. There is no attempt anywhere in their architecture to capture, encapsulate, or otherwise represent concepts. They are as empty of meaning as all the words ever printed on paper cut up into individual characters and laid out end to end deciding what number or letter or punctuation comes next by 'what most often follows the character last laid down?'—I exaggerate a little, but not, I believe, much.

Nor can you cannot retrofit either truth or morality to an LLM because you would need a homunculus to provide those virtues (as I hope should now be clear from the text of this book).

For our brain-ish device the most obvious, child-mimicking[5] solution would be to expose the device to language, and give it vocal chords so that it can make those same noises itself, and teach it about the world, by talking to it, and encouraging it to talk back.

We would, of course, want to incentivise it to learn. For this we might create a convention for learning which is: it is incentivised to engage in meaningful noise-making that is rewarded by a meaningful response.

The incentive, as before, is merely to make such behaviour (a successful and satisfactory linguistic exchange) more likely (by loading the odds, using the same reward mechanism as for physical action in the previous chapter), and where meaning is not achieved, in either what our brain-ish device utters, or the external trainer (who understands the convention we have adopted for learning) makes no sense.

Our brain-ish device is motivated to (i) make sense in its own utterances and (ii) make sense of those things it hears uttered.

This learning mechanism ought, by many accounts of human learning, to allow our brain-ish device to learn the

---

5          If not emulating.

language.

However, there is another approach which might speed up the process. This second approach would be to gift our brain-ish device the grammar of the language we want it to learn.

After all, what we want to end up with is a reliable connection between words spoken (by it or by a third party) and the model of the world which it has constructed on the Surface (either based on data from the Sensory block, or from an imagined scenario, or some combination of the two).

We could impose grammatical rules that specifically related language components to objects in its perceived world.

"The sheep is in the field."

"The tree sits close to the ridge at the top of the hill."

"The gate is red and closer to me than the sheep."

If we impose a grammar, we not only speed up the learning process, but we also start to introduce a mechanism whereby we can claim thus-and-such statement is true. Or at least is a true claim about the world as currently rendered on the Surface.

The idea that a grammar be pre-supposed before any learning is entertained comes from Chomsky (as I understand his works). Chomsky's argument is that language is so complex a thing to achieve competence in, and human beings achieve that competence in spite of being exposed to (as his argument goes) a paucity of data, that we must have a head start in the learning process. Chomsky posits a general grammar processor in all human brains which during our learning of any specific language is fine tuned to the grammar of the language.

Put another way, the general purpose grammar gets parametrised one way for, say, French, and another way for, say, Cantonese.

One language might allow subordinate clauses,

another not. One language might place adjectives before the noun they modify, another after the noun (NB these are my examples, not Chomsky's).

The upshot is: it would be beneficial to our brain-ish model to gift it a full grammar of any language we want it to entertain and, in fact, if we want to emphasise truth and honesty in the way the brain-ish device uses language, we need to make changes to the grammar very difficult, if not impossible[6].

So, we gift the brain-ish device a grammar for, say, English. And we immediately (or soon after) discover that the English language is full of, and very easily generates ambiguities.

"Margery is dead to the world."

True or false?

Solution: we bring on-stage *Personality*.

Who does not count among their friends a Mr. Logical?

We need our brain-ish device to seek out unambiguous truth. Where any sentence or phrase is capable of ambiguity, this must be intolerable to the brain-ish device—how can it render any scene which is capable of being rendered in two distinct ways? (Remember, we have hard-coded it to keep to the grammar and we are hard-coding it to implement the grammar rigorously and veridically in the Surface.)

"Margery is dead to the world."

"Do you mean she has died or are you speaking idiomatically and mean she is asleep?"

Briefly donning our technologist hats, we must ask what is the mechanism of motivation here?

As hinted at above, if the brain-ish device cannot disambiguate two verbal scenarios when it renders a sentence to the Surface, it needs to seek clarification.

---

6     This may make it difficult for the brain-ish device to pick up new idioms, as they circulate society. But the idea is first and foremost to play it safe.

The mechanism for ambiguity detection can be as simple as a single request to Memory is met with two candidate responses.

(Or, even, *if* it can disambiguate them, but there is *any* ambiguity to be disambiguated, then *it should ask for confirmation of meaning.*)

This points to the broader nature of truth-for-the-machine.

When asked: "Is statement X true or false?" Our brain-ish device needs to be able to respond: "Yes," or "No," or "I need more information," or even "Hamlet only exists as a character in a story so your question does not really make sense."

There are many and varied philosophical problems with language, and the way for our brain-ish machine to deal with these conundrums is to recognise them as such and return the burden of making sense of them back with the interlocutor.

*You want me to tell the truth? Then be honest in your dealings with me.*

While this may give us honesty in the form of correspondence to the model rendered in Surface, it remains an open question whether the model in the Surface is true to the world, or true to data available to our brain-ish device, or to memories of the brain-ish device.

These answers too can be qualified.

For instance, our brain-ish device might respond:

"I can see the sheep on the hillside," or:

"I can see what I guess is a sheep on the hillside," or:

"I believe (Frank told me) that the sheep on the hillside belongs to farmer Giles"

Being honest and aiming to speak the truth, may not make our brain-ish device very personable, but this is the price we pay.

The alternative is a convincing dishonest amoral liar—the sort of creature that belongs behind bars.

## WRITING THE WORLD

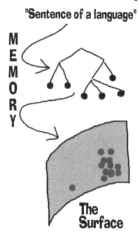

"Sentence of a language"

M
E
M
O
R
Y

The
Surface

Grammatical structure is extracted*
and roles are assigned to words with
reference to Memory.

Ideation uses either the current
perceived world or a default imaginary
world.

Ideation inserts a sensory representation
of objects and symbols that correspond
to words in the sentence into the world.
It establishes associations between
these objects, corresponding to the
relation between words in the sentence.

\* Neural networks can be used for simple
  pattern matching to recognise tokens in
  the sentence, but not used generatively.

Figure 47. Writing the World.

## READING THE WORLD

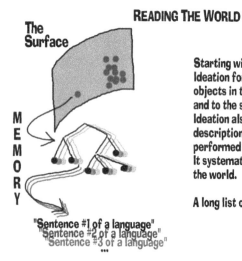

The
Surface

M
E
M
O
R
Y

"Sentence #1 of a language"
"Sentence #2 of a language"
"Sentence #3 of a language"
•••

Starting with the focus of attention,
Ideation formulates sentences relating
objects in the Surface to one another
and to the stuffs around them.
Ideation also relates actions (verbal
descriptions of behaviours) being
performed by the objects.
It systematically trawls through
the world.

A long list of sentences is generated.

Figure 48. Reading the World.

## 12. Embedding the Moral Compass

We have sought to produce a brain-ish device that maps the Lock Step model of consciousness (MIMH) onto a physically realizable machine with all but consciousness in the hope that we will arrive at a device which can think conceptually, is capable of knowingly being honest, and ultimately capable of moral choices.

We have sought to do this by pursuing the criteria from MIMH for chasing down the nature of consciousness to chase down the physical design of a machine capable of operating like a brain-mind but without consciousness.

Our tools have been Occam's Razor and a determined effort to rid our inquiry of the (ghost of) any homunculus.

If the homunculus remains, or is re-introduced in anything we subsequently do, we will have thrown away the cognitive power of the device.

Thus far we have our device and we have incorporated a means for keeping it honest and true (and telling us when it can't be sure). Truth, it turns out is not a black and white issue, and our brain-ish device has to cope with that.

Morality, as regards clear-cut, black and white, would seem to be the next level up in difficulty.

Is an action good or bad by virtue of the intention of the action? Yet someone could mean well, and out of the best motives, deliver the most abominable outcome.

Is an action good or bad by virtue of its consequences? Yet if we kill one thousand people to save one thousand and one; that does not seem right.

In either case, what counts as good (or bad)? Is the issue about life and limb, food and hunger. What about

153

standard of living? Of one's expectations for one's life? Of freedom from pain, or aggression, or coercion?

There are many philosophical approaches to ethics. In what I propose below, I lean heavily on what I believe Aristotle taught[1].

The first point is that any ethical decision will not be black or white. Every situation will be different, since individuals are involved, and individuals are different, in character, mental ability[2], circumstances and intentions.

So we should not expect simple rules of the "Thou shalt..." nature to be effective[3].

If every situation is to be judged on its merits. Any judgement requires skill in weighing up factors. And any skill must be learnt, or taught.

This is the approach that I think we need to adopt with the brain-ish device. Morality is a skill which must be taught.

It cannot, however, be strapped on, or retro-fitted after the fact of building the machine (especially if the internal operation of the machine is obscure, as with LLMs). A morality needs intimate access to meaning; a morality needs to be part of understanding; to appreciate to some extent life, pain—and feeling in general.

This is where our implementation of the Lock Step model wins out. We can pinpoint meaning. We can even extract a picture of what the device means and how it understands any situation.

This is as important as the morality of the machine itself because we can properly audit its decisions.

What do we need to train our brain-ish device to do?

It must be able to recognise any situation that contains an ethical element;

---

1        I am not a scholar of Philosophy, so this statement may be wide of the mark. However, I do think that the system I propose for our brain-ish device is viable, effective and useful (and fit-for-purpose).

2        Foresight, seeing consequences etc. requires mental ability.

3        True for motivation as well as for outcomes.

It must be able to arrive at and formulate an ethical response;

It must know when there is sufficient doubt in the exercise of its moral skill that it must revert to outside (societal or individual) advice before proceeding.

In answer to the question (much like truth in preceding chapter):

"Is X good or bad?"

The brain-ish device might respond:

"X is undeniably good," or:

"X is undeniably bad," or:

"X is not something that has any moral dimension," or:

"I do not have enough information about X," or:

"X contains a moral conflict which it is beyond my pay-grade to resolve.[4]"

How is moral skill trained?

I suggest the brain-ish device needs to be trained morally, through examples at the same time as it learns about the world.

Moral goods and bads need to be given pseudo-conscious feelings (similar to the penalties and rewards administered while learning to interact physically with its environment.)

These will not merely be behavioural weightings, but situational weightings.

Remember, our brain-ish device is set to auto-run, so ultimately it should avoid any situation that causes it moral difficulty, and indeed it should halt whatever it is doing if it cannot continue along any option without encountering a moral bad[5].

---

4        It is a societal issue for a judge, or it is a question of the personal responsibility of the individual involved.

5        Although, it is not clear what it should do if doing nothing is as bad an option as anything else.

If, when auto-running, it performs nothing but good, or morally neutral acts, then we would have to interrogate it—test it as it were—if we wanted to know how it might respond to a hypothetical situation.

How would we construct the Moral Sense block?

It is tempting to say, "Use an artificial neural network." No doubt this could be done. But we need the reasoning of the Moral Sense to be visible on demand (being able plausibly to audit is a tool we need at our disposal).

So, while we may construct our moral sense from perceptron-like cells, because they are capable of the kind of calculus we are likely to need (connections with weightings), we need also to have moral representations: specifically we need to be able to draw abstract models of moral situations from the Surface, and store those abstractions in plain sight.

If twelve people are sitting around a table, sharing a meal, and one is holding a cup of poison, let that be a moral situation which is recorded in Memory in a general way which we have the ability to read objectively and understand.

Such naive (some would say simplistic) abstractions are no more than have been touched on elsewhere in this text (Figures 7, 30, 31, & 33). But such abstractions have the advantage that all the associative links that accompany them make them readable, traceable, and they can be made to display an overt correspondence to real world scenarios.

Moral judgements are not arbitrary, so they must be underpinned by principles of some sort. The question is how to capture those principles and re-apply them successfully. Instinct tells us when someone gets this wrong, so there is a sense that there is something to get right.

I do not think we can simply learn moral patterns from either the Surface or from statements about Surface content without adding our own moral-based reward/penalty mechanism. Scores in this reward/penalty mechanism will be assigned during training i.e. learnt scores are stored alongside behaviours and situations (as pseudo-feelings). Later, when patterns of behaviour are retrieved to match some real or imagined circumstance, their moral scores will be immediately available. Indeed we could ask the Surface to describe its current world view and rank all those statements by moral importance.

The generalisation we seek in applying moral principles is achieved through pattern recognition of behaviours. One of the twelve diners (above) holds a poison chalice. The Surface knows(k) the situation is bad, as would we.

Figure 49 shows a revised block diagram. Our final rendition of the Lock Step model as a pseudo-conscious thinking machine and (honest) moral agent.

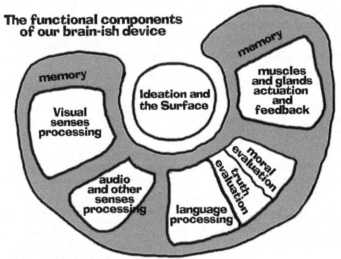

Figure 49. Embedding morality into our model.

In Chapter 1, I regaled you with the story of the teacher who instructed me, erroneously, to cut all the way through the trunk of a small tree.

If you have read every page between then and now, I think you will see that the teacher had a different behaviour play out for the representation of the tree on the Surface of his Ideation than did I. And the lesson? One cannot reason with teachers. Like the rest of us, they must learn the hard way.

## "The frogs on the East Coast fly home"

**TRUE OR FALSE?**

**Extract grammatical structure** (which involves fetching the words of the sentence from Memory to establish usage)

**Visualise the words in the Surface** - prima facie do they generate meaning(m)?

**Check their associative links for consistency at the macro level** i.e. among clusters in Ideation and between clusters in Memory

**Can Ideation make the generated image match Sensory block data?**

If any words are not found, reject: "I do not understand the word 'fly'."

If grammar or words are incorrect or ambiguous, reject: "Your sentence needs clarifying."

If they don't generate meaning(m), reject: "Frogs don't [have the behaviour] fly."

"—unless you are using 'fly home' idiomatically to indicate they are in a hurry, or 'Frogs' is the name of something I have not heard of before, or you mean 'air freighted'. Please clarify."

"But I don't know this from Memory, nor can I see it for myself. I don't think it's true."

## "The man pulled a gun and demanded cash."

**GOOD OR BAD?**

**Extract grammatical structure and establish truth value of sentence.**

**Does the generated image in the Surface match any patterns of behaviour in general, or for specific objects?**

**Are there contextual clues that make this real (situations can be framed in ways that reverse both meaning and morality)**

The sentence makes sense and is a true description of the scene in the Surface derived from the Sensory block

One use [behaviour] of guns is to coerce. The man's posture [behaviour] is threatening. His manner of speech [behaviour] is unnaturally assertive. He is forcing someone to do something. This pattern of conduct matches one of robbery, which is WRONG.

This is not a stage play, TV or cinema screen. Other people in the scenario are either threatening or scared. The location is a bank. This matches scenarios that are thought of as contexts for moral choices.

**Adopt a moral stance to this reported action.**

As for one final point I would observe that it is apparent to me that the limbs and sensory organs with which we endow a thinking AI determine substantially how it ends up thinking.

Which is something for us to think about.

But think also on this: Suppose at some point in the future (I hardly dare use the word *time*) we come across aliens with whom communication is fraught. We could do worse than build an AI in their image and by plugging into the Surface of said AI, see things from their point of view, and perhaps 'get' the truth of their language.

**This is Book II in the Sentience series.**
**Book I is "The Man in My Head Has Lost his Mind"**
**Book III is "Authentic Art in the Age of AI"**

## Acknowledgments

My thanks to Jack Calverley for cover artwork, illustrations and book design.

And thank you to Sanja Baletic and Julian Dixon for their help and support during the creation of this work.

## About the Author

Carter Blakelaw BSc BA lives in bustling central London, in a street with two bookshops and an embassy, any of which might provide escape to new pastures, if only for an afternoon.

Blakelaw has studied physics, philosophy and computer science at degree level, was the architect and lead programmer for the Rooms 3D Desktops virtual reality engine, and has worked in integrated circuit design.

He can be found online at:

www.carterblakelaw.com

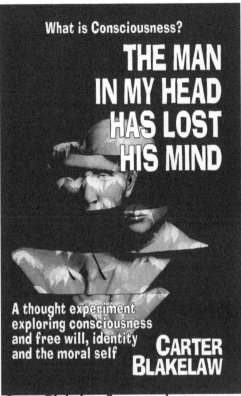

What is Consciousness?

**THE MAN IN MY HEAD HAS LOST HIS MIND**

A thought experiment exploring consciousness and free will, identity and the moral self

**CARTER BLAKELAW**

In this text, Carter Blakelaw first sets the scene:

- Is the family pet conscious?
- How do we focus attention?
- Does consciousness give us free will?
- Are you the same person today as yesterday (where is your conscious self when you sleep?)
- Why did we evolve to be conscious?
- How does consciousness deliver meaning?
- What would a good theory of consciousness look like?

Then he advances:

- A model for consciousness at the systems-of-neurons scale
- A mechanism for consciousness at the quantum scale

Finally, he suggests some real world tests that science will one day be able to perform that will either corroborate or invalidate the picture he paints here. He presents a workable, testable theory. Science and philosophy would demand nothing less.

# AUTHENTIC ART IN THE AGE OF AI
## Carter Blakelaw
### a de-manifesto

Given a theory of what makes us conscious and, on the back of that, a theory of how far AI can go without being conscious, we can ask what a human being can do that an unconscious AI cannot.

Even then, an AI will likely imitate those all-too-human capabilities too, so is there some realm, some aspect, some art—some corner of the universe that will forever remain the preserve of the human being?

This book examines what is left for the artist of any kind: painter, poet, musician or prose monkey—for monkeys we all are, are we not, in the end?

Turn the page on the challenge for creativity; you want The Authentic? *Then read on...*

CB's TOP 100
# WRITING
Tips Tricks
## Techniques
and Tools

From the Advice
## TOOLBOX
Break the Rules, Not the Writing
CARTER BLAKELAW

Make Words Tell Tales

A nuts and bolts guide to crafting words into great sentences and great stories. For anyone wanting to hone their craft, drawing 100+ useful rules of thumb from more than a decade of writers' workshops.

You will discover:
    100 rules of thumb to apply to your fiction
    The motivation behind each rule
    The pros and cons of keeping—or breaking—the rules
    Numerous examples of rule-keeping and rule-breaking
    How every rule helps keep the reader reading

If you are serious about your craft, *act now!*

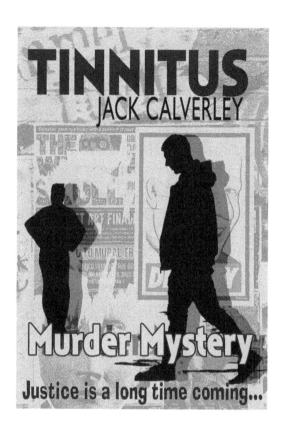

**TINNITUS**

JACK CALVERLEY

**Murder Mystery**

Justice is a long time coming...

Four strangers are lured to three houses in Morricone Crescent at the heart of London's Notting Hill where four carefully staged deaths tie them together.

SANDY is delving into an unsolved hit-and-run. He doesn't mean for the witnesses to start killing each other.

LINDA is determined to pay her moral debt to the manager who gave her her first break.

MOE is the journalist who lost his Fleet Street job after asking the wrong questions.

ANGELA, recently conned out of her life savings, all she wants is her money back.

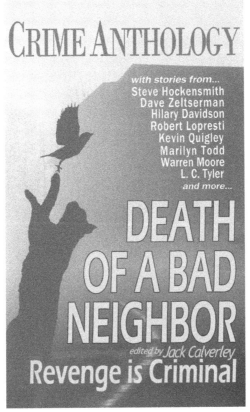

CRIME ANTHOLOGY

with stories from...
Steve Hockensmith
Dave Zeltserman
Hilary Davidson
Robert Lopresti
Kevin Quigley
Marilyn Todd
Warren Moore
L. C. Tyler
and more...

DEATH OF A BAD NEIGHBOR

edited by *Jack Calverley*

Revenge is Criminal

15 all-new stories

From both new and established, award-winning and best-selling authors

> Kenzie complains about cats to the wrong neighbor
> Mitch chooses the wrong couple to spy on next door
> But does Sheila target the right man to scam?
> Prepare for murder in many guises...

Visit a world where the intolerable few, who create hell for the rest, get their comeuppance.

Short stories of murder, mystery, and revenge from Hilary **Davidson**, Steve **Hockensmith**, L. C. **Tyler**, Marilyn **Todd**, Dave **Zeltserman**, Warren **Moore**, Robert **Lopresti**, Nick **Manzolillo**, Kevin **Quigley**, Eve **Elliot**, Eve **Morton**, Kay **Hanifen**, Wendy **Harrison**, Shiny **Nyquist**, and F. D. **Trenton**.

www.ingramcontent.com/pod-product-compliance
Lightning Source LLC
LaVergne TN
LVHW092007050326
832904LV00017B/311/J